FAITH REWARDED

**A PERSONAL ACCOUNT OF PROPHETIC
PROMISES TO THE EAST GERMAN SAINTS**

FROM THE JOURNAL OF

THOMAS S. MONSON

Deseret Book Company
Salt Lake City, Utah

Library of Congress Cataloging-in-Publication Data

Monson, Thomas S., 1927–
    Faith rewarded : a personal account of prophetic promises to the East German saints / by Thomas S. Monson.
        p.   cm.
    Includes index.
    ISBN 1-57345-186-X
    1. Monson, Thomas S., 1927– Diaries. 2. Mormons—Germany (East)— Biography. 3. Missionaries—Germany (East)—Biography. 4. Missionaries—United States—Biography. 5. Church of Jesus Christ of Latter-day Saints—Germany (East)—History—Sources. 6. Mormon Church—Germany (East)—History—Sources. 7. Germany (East)—Church history—20th century—Sources. I. Title.
BX8695.M56A3   1996
289.3'431'09045—dc20   96-8147
                                                                     CIP

Printed in the United States of America

10   9   8   7   6   5   4   3   2   1

CONTENTS

INTRODUCTION

In July 1968, about five years after my call to the Quorum of the Twelve Apostles, I was assigned to supervise the European missions of the Church. It was this assignment that took me to East Germany, which was then under strict Communist rule, to visit the Saints who lived behind the Iron Curtain.

I wish it were possible to fully describe conditions in East Germany at the time when I first traveled there. The Communist party's hammer-and-sickle flag was displayed in each window of the ancient and war-ravaged hotel where I stayed. Church meetings were watched and monitored by the secret police. East German citizens were not allowed to leave their country without special permission from the government, and such permission was seldom granted. The feeling in East Germany was one of overwhelming oppression, with evidence of Communist rule all around.

I discovered that departure from East Germany was usually a day-long process, even for those of us who presented U.S. passports. Cement barriers, arranged in a zigzag fashion, had been erected in order to prevent drivers from using their vehicles to make a dash for freedom. We drove from one guard post to the next while East German police checked our passports and searched our vehicle. Some used mirrors to check the undercarriage of our car for stowaway passengers.

In the midst of this seemingly gloomy atmosphere, the

faith and goodness of the East German Latter-day Saints was a welcome beacon. I was deeply moved by their plight, and as I addressed them in Görlitz late in 1968, I felt prompted to promise them that if they would remain true and faithful, every blessing enjoyed by Church members in any other country would be theirs. In April 1975, I offered a prayer to rededicate the land of East Germany, and in that prayer, specific blessings were requested and promises made. I felt prompted to promise the Saints that the day of the rededication of their land would be the dawning of a new beginning. I asked the Lord to open up the way to His holy temple. I pled that East German youth would be allowed to serve missions in other lands. Other blessings were promised, including the Lord's intervention in governmental affairs. At the time, it seemed nearly impossible that such blessings would ever come to the oppressed East German Saints. But I knew them to be good people, and I felt a reassurance that these things would come to pass if they remained faithful.

When my friends Thelma and Percy Fetzer learned I had been assigned to supervise the European missions, Thelma said to me, "Tom, I know you to be a good man, but when you come back from the German Democratic Republic, having met with our members there, you will be an even better man." In the twenty-eight years during which I have had close association with the people of the former East Germany, I have seen this to be true. Again and again my testimony has been strengthened as I have met with these good Saints and have heard and recorded fragments of their life stories.

Much of my recording has been in the form of personal journal entries highlighting my experiences with the East German Saints. *Faith Rewarded* is a collection of those entries, extracted from my personal journal. The earliest entry is dated July 12, 1968, and the most recent, August 27, 1995. I have not felt it necessary to add intervening text between the entries, which are arranged chronologically.

It is my hope that as you read these leaves from my journal, you will gain greater love and appreciation for a people who remained faithful in adversity, prayed fervently for the full blessings of the gospel, and were eventually rewarded with miraculous answers to their humble prayers.

1

Behind the Iron Curtain

MY FIRST VISITS TO EAST GERMANY 1968–69

FRIDAY, JULY 12, 1968

Met this morning with Hartman Rector, Jr. Together we have been assigned to supervise the work of the missions in Germany and Italy, as well as Austria and Switzerland.

WEDNESDAY, JULY 31, 1968

Flew to Berlin and visited behind the Iron Curtain in East Berlin. This is my first visit to the German Democratic Republic, or East Germany. Prior to my coming, my wife, Frances, and I had been reading about Americans being arrested in East Germany and held as spies. Frances said to me, "Are you really going to go there?"

I answered, "Yes, I am going. Would you like to go with me?"

She replied, "Tom, we have children to raise. You go, and I will stay here and watch the children. Then if you don't come back, they will have one of us to give them guidance!"

I said, "All right; pray for me."

What a stark contrast as one passes through Checkpoint Charlie and finds freedom snuffed out and Communism

1

dominating all. Machine guns, soldiers, and German shepherd dogs were everywhere.

Stanley D. Rees, president of the Germany Hamburg Mission, and I visited the Soviet War Memorial there. We were happy, however, to return to the West and to cross back into an island of freedom—namely, West Berlin. It is tragic to note the wreath marking the persons who have lost their lives trying to escape over the Berlin Wall.

We stayed the night in Berlin and enjoyed walking in the streets of this city, which has been almost completely rebuilt. In contrast to East Berlin, where the results of bombing and shelling in World War II are everywhere to be seen, West Berlin is practically a new city. An old church, however, bore stark evidence of the bombing which had destroyed part of it, the ruins left intact as a memorial.

FRIDAY, NOVEMBER 8, 1968

Flew from Palermo, Sicily, to Milan, Italy, where the plane landed in a dense fog. After some delay I was able to make my connection to Zurich and thence to Frankfurt and Berlin. In Berlin I was met by President Stanley Rees, president of the Germany Hamburg Mission, and joined Elder Hartman Rector and others in a meeting of all the missionaries in the general Berlin area.

SATURDAY, NOVEMBER 9, 1968

Joined President and Sister Stanley Rees for our trip to East Germany. We crossed Checkpoint Charlie into the East Zone and after considerable delay with government officials were able to receive a tourist visa which permitted us to journey on to Görlitz. En route we passed through an agricultural area in East Germany. I was surprised to note

Faithful members of the Görlitz Branch, which met in this battered building, longed for the day when the full program and blessings of the gospel would be theirs.

that all farm machinery was horse-drawn. Not one tractor did I see. The weather was cold and foggy; hence, a very dismal atmosphere pervaded the scene. The autobahns were void of traffic, indicating the scarcity of automobiles in East Germany. We paused at Dresden, Germany, and I recalled that this city had the reputation of being one of the most heavily bombed cities of any during World War II. In one evening Allied bombs took the lives of three hundred thousand people.

It was raining when we arrived in Görlitz. We went to the local hotel, which was the most archaic of any hotel I have yet seen. My room had ceilings fifteen feet high, with a bed that resembled a box and a sink which was ancient in vintage. The room was cold, and a Communist flag graced the window. Lavatory facilities existed only on the second floor of the hotel, and these were most inadequate. Communism has nothing to offer as a competitor to the free enterprise system.

SUNDAY, NOVEMBER 10, 1968

Met this morning with the German Saints in the Dresden District—my first meeting with the Saints in the German Democratic Republic. A marvelous spirit prevailed. My, how the German Saints can sing the hymns of Zion! One of the songs was especially beautiful and so meaningful when one considers the humble circumstances of these wonderful people. Following are the words:

> If the way be full of trial; Weary not!
> If it's one of sore denial, Weary not!
> If it now be one of weeping,
> There will come a joyous greeting,
> When the harvest we are reaping—Weary not!

> (Chorus)
> Do not weary by the way,
> Whatever be thy lot;
> There awaits a brighter day
> To all, to all who weary not!

> If the way be one of sorrow, Weary not!
> Happier will be the morrow, Weary not!
> Here we suffer tribulation,
> Here we must endure temptation;
> But there'll come a great salvation—Weary not!

> If misfortune overtake us, Weary not!
> Jesus never will forsake us, Weary not!

4

He will leave us never, never,
From His love there's naught can sever;
Glory to the Lamb forever!—Weary not!
> (*Deseret Sunday School Songs* [Salt Lake City:
> Deseret Sunday School Union, 1909], no. 158)

These members love the scriptures. I learned that they have almost no written manuals or materials—just the standard works. Yet they are so well informed. This says something about concentrating one's reading in the standard works.

I was touched by the sincerity of these wonderful Saints. I was humbled by their poverty. They have so little. My heart filled with sorrow because they have no patriarch, they have no wards or stakes—just branches, they have few teaching materials. They cannot receive temple blessings, neither endowments nor sealings. They are forbidden to leave their country. Yet they trust in the Lord with all their hearts and lean not unto their own understanding.

I stood at the pulpit with tear-filled eyes and a voice choked with emotion and made a promise to the people: "If you will remain true and faithful to the commandments of God, every blessing any member of the Church enjoys in any other country will be yours." Although this was a dramatic promise, I believe it was inspired by our Heavenly Father and will be fulfilled under His direction as the Saints in the German Democratic Republic continue to demonstrate their faith.

This was the first time, to my knowledge, that a General Authority has visited Görlitz, and it has been many years since the Dresden District itself was visited by one of the Brethren. There were 235 persons in attendance.

Following the general sessions, we met at length with Brother Henry Burkhardt, Brother Stanley Rees's counselor with specific responsibility for the portion of the mission behind the Iron Curtain.

Following the conferences, we returned to Berlin, providing transportation for Sister Edith Krause, who was to meet her son Helaman at Berlin. Sister Krause mentioned a faith-promoting experience I should like to record:

She indicated that toward the end of World War II, when the Russian troops were invading the city, the branch president brought the Church records to her and said, "Protect these, and the Lord will protect you." He was fearful that his home would be searched most carefully. Sister Krause mentioned that she lived on the third floor of an apartment building. The Russians, upon entering the city, ransacked the first two floors of the apartment building and were headed up the stairs to the third floor when, miraculously, their leader called them back and they went on their way to another block. Sister Krause and the records remained safe.

At Berlin we approached our rendezvous point and noticed Helaman Krause in the car awaiting our arrival. There was not a heater in the car, and he had a blanket about him to keep warm. I learned that this nineteen-year-old son of Walter Krause had been offered a full scholarship to the university if he would but join the Communist Youth Party. He declined and said that he would prefer paying his own way. He would not have been granted entrance to the university except for the fact that his grade point average was the highest in his entire high school. I came away wishing it were possible for him to fill a full-time mission, but such will not be the case at this particular time.

As I produced my U.S. passport to gain entrance into West Germany, I felt grateful for the fact that I live in a free country. I don't know when a passport has meant so much to me as when I came to realize that this document was the only thing that distinguished between me—with the freedom and privileges which I enjoy—and my brothers and sisters behind the Iron Curtain, with the lack of freedom which is their unhappy lot.

When our dear friends Thelma and Percy Fetzer learned I had been assigned to supervise the missions in Europe, including the area of East Germany, Thelma said to me, "Tom, I know you to be a good man, but when you come back from the German Democratic Republic, having met with our members there, you will be an even better man." I testify that this is true. Percy formerly served as president of the Germany Hamburg Mission, which mission has responsibility for the work in East Germany.

This evening in my hotel room, as I realized the full impact of the promise I had made at Görlitz earlier today, I dropped to my knees and said to my Heavenly Father, "Father, I am on Thy errand; this is Thy Church. I have spoken words that came not from me, but from Thee and Thy Son. Wilt Thou, therefore, fulfill the promise in the lives of this noble people." There coursed through my mind the words from the Psalm, "Be still, and know that I am God" (Psalm 46:10).

FRIDAY, JUNE 13, 1969

I departed Frankfurt early in the morning en route to Berlin. Frances and the children remained in Frankfurt.

In Berlin I was met by President and Sister Stanley Rees, they having flown to Berlin in company with Percy and Thelma Fetzer. We decided to drive but one car into East Germany. After a three-hour delay at the border obtaining

7

visas, hotel accommodations, etc., we proceeded on our way to the city of Dresden.

One realizes immediately upon crossing the border that he is in a land where freedom is curtailed and tyranny exalted. Hundreds upon hundreds of tiny shops were closed, with state-operated stores substituting for them. Long lines could be seen at any grocery store. I noticed that the commodities seemed highly inferior to ours and yet cost the poor people such an exorbitant price.

Upon arrival in Dresden we went directly to the hotel, where we spent the evening.

SATURDAY, JUNE 14, 1969

Early this morning we drove to the place of meeting in Dresden. Everywhere we noticed Russian troops and East German troops. We were amazed to find that a barracks housing Russian soldiers is located just adjacent to our meetinghouse, with the German Secret Police a short distance away. We parked the car several blocks from the place of meeting and walked in pairs to the chapel.

At the chapel we met with Henry Burkhardt, one of the most faithful Latter-day Saints I have ever met. Truly the Lord has raised him up to help provide for the Saints in East Germany.

In accordance with approval granted by the First Presidency and the Council of the Twelve, all of the membership in East Germany, or the German Democratic Republic, were organized into the Dresden Mission, with Johannes Henry Burkhardt being ordained a high priest and set apart as president. He selected as his counselors Erich Walter Krause and Gottfried Richter. I invited Percy Fetzer and Stanley Rees to join me in setting apart these brethren.

On June 14, 1969, the Dresden Mission is organized. Front row, left to right: Erich Walter Krause, Mission President Johannes Henry Burkhardt, and Gottfried Richter make up the presidency of the Dresden Mission. Back row, left to right: Elder Thomas S. Monson, Percy K. Fetzer, and Stanley D. Rees.

President Burkhardt had any information we needed at his fingertips. He was in a position to answer any question we would ask relative to the activity of the Church. His counselor, Brother Krause, likewise has been a most faithful and fearless member of the Church and has risked imprisonment many times for his actions in behalf of Church members.

Printing and publishing are absolutely forbidden in East Germany, nor are supplies permitted from the West. Therefore, the only way we can furnish information to our various branches for courses of study is to manually type any lesson, making three carbon copies. Carbon paper is at a premium and is sometimes impossible to procure. With

Three faithful brethren served as the presidency of the Dresden Mission. Left to right: Erich Walter Krause, President Johannes Henry Burkhardt, and Gottfried Richter.

forty-seven branches, this means that every lesson for a given class would have to be typewritten twelve times. Through the divine providence of our Heavenly Father, Brother Richter has been permitted to operate his own stationery store, which is almost unheard of in a collective society. This enables the Church to obtain all the carbon paper needed for our Church operation in East Germany.

Today will go down as a day of historic importance for the Saints in Germany.

This evening we joined in a testimony meeting which marked the termination of a five-day genealogical workshop. The membership of the Church in East Germany had pledged to provide ten thousand names for the Church Genealogical Society prior to June 20. The purpose of the five-day seminar was to work diligently in recording these names. At the termination of the period, not ten thousand names were provided, but rather, fourteen thousand names. A glorious spirit permeated the testimony meeting.

When we returned to the hotel at 9:30 P.M., we realized that we had been working continuously and steadily since 7:30 A.M. I don't know of a day in my life when so much good has been accomplished.

SUNDAY, JUNE 15, 1969

Attended a leadership meeting of the branch presidencies and district presidencies of the Dresden Mission. Out of a total possible attendance of 87, there were 84 present. President Burkhardt had prepared some material from the new *General Handbook of Instructions,* which material was received enthusiastically by the branch and district presidents. These people delight in following detailed instructions to the very letter.

The use of the new handbook reminded me of an experience I had not long ago. I had just completed an assignment pertaining to the revision of the *General Handbook of Instructions*—a slow, detailed, three-year project. While in the temple one Thursday morning, I said to Elder Spencer W. Kimball, "With all my heart I wish we had one copy of the newly completed German-language edition of the handbook available in the German Democratic Republic."

Brother Kimball said, "Why can't you simply mail one?"

I replied, "The importation of such literature is forbidden. There is no way."

Then he said, "I have an idea, Brother Monson. Why don't you, since you have worked with the handbook, memorize it; and then we'll put *you* across the border!"

I laughed and then looked at Brother Kimball. He was not laughing; he was serious. The man meant what he said. I began the difficult assignment of attempting to memorize the handbook. I did not commit it to memory; I lack that capacity. But I pretty well had the paragraphs, the chapters, and the pages, with their content, stored away in my memory.

When I crossed the border to East Berlin, I said to our leader there, "Give me a typewriter and a ream of paper and let me work." When all was provided, I sat down at a table in the branch office and began to type the handbook. I was about thirty pages into it when I took time to stand and stretch. I noticed on a shelf what appeared to be the *General Handbook of Instructions*. I retrieved the volume and discovered that it was, indeed, the new handbook, printed in the German language. I felt all my efforts had been in vain, but I now have a good recall of the handbook.

A few statistics about the Saints in East Germany: They total 4,641 in number and are situated in 47 branches and 7 member districts. In 1968 there were 47 baptisms, of which 17 were convert baptisms. Percentages for sacrament meeting attendance, home teaching, and other activities of the Church are far higher than in West Germany or in the other stakes of Europe.

The Saints rejoiced when Thelma Fetzer spoke to them about the Primary, she being a member of the Primary general board; and when Percy Fetzer gave them detailed instructions pertaining to the priesthood programs of the Church, they were most receptive. Truly Percy and Thelma are loved and revered in Germany as well as here at home. President and Sister Rees were likewise well received.

Following the leadership conference, we attended the Sunday School and sacrament meeting of the Dresden Branch, after which we concluded our business in East Germany and returned to Berlin.

As we crossed Checkpoint Charlie and arrived in West Berlin, we thanked God once again for our blessings. We remembered that earlier Friday morning, as we had prepared to go across the border, at my invitation President Stanley Rees had supplicated the Lord that the guards would be blinded to our true purpose. As we went across the border, we were among the very few who were not asked to open their suitcases so the guards could make a detailed inspection of all the contents being transported.

TUESDAY, JULY 1, 1969

Today I met with Brother Percy K. Fetzer relative to matters in East Germany. Invited to the meeting were the superintendencies and presidencies of the auxiliary organizations and Elder Hartman Rector. We made preliminary arrangements for the auxiliary officers in turn to accompany Brother Fetzer to East Germany. It will be a glorious thing for the Saints behind the Iron Curtain to have a greater portion of the full program of the Church.

WEDNESDAY, JULY 23, 1969

This afternoon I had the privilege of meeting Percy K. Fetzer and his wife Thelma. I advised them that the First Presidency and Council of the Twelve had approved the recommendation that Percy be ordained a patriarch and authorized to provide patriarchal blessings to worthy Saints in

Eastern Europe. I ordained Percy to this office in the priesthood. It was a thrilling and momentous occasion for all of us.

Following my visit last month to East Germany, as I reported to the First Presidency and Twelve, I expressed my sorrow at the inability of so many of our Saints living there to receive their patriarchal blessings. I mentioned that although Brother Karl Ringger, an ordained patriarch from Switzerland, had been able to journey behind the Iron Curtain to provide some blessings, the vast majority who desire patriarchal blessings have as yet been unable to receive them. President David O. McKay said to me, "Brother Monson, whom did you say accompanied you on this visit?"

"I was with Brother Percy K. Fetzer, our Regional Representative," I replied.

President McKay asked, "Is he a good man?"

My response: "Among the finest!"

Then President McKay said, "Why don't you ordain him a patriarch, and then each time he goes into that area, he can give patriarchal blessings to the worthy Saints there."

Thus, Percy has today been ordained a patriarch. What a blessing this will be for our dear members in Eastern Europe.

2

"Weary Not!"

**FAITHFUL EAST GERMAN SAINTS
1970–73**

Held an early-morning meeting with the missionaries of the Germany North Mission who are laboring in the Berlin area. The building was cold, inasmuch as no one had advised the custodian to turn on the heat. We improvised, however, by moving into a smaller room. A choice spirit prevailed as the missionaries bore testimony and otherwise demonstrated to me their devotion to the gospel and desire to do the work of the Lord.

Following this meeting, President and Sister Eugene Bryson and I drove through Checkpoint Charlie and, after passing the border guards four times, drove through a drizzling rainstorm for four and one-half hours to the city of Erfurt, where we stayed at the Erfurter Hof Hotel.

After we had checked into the hotel, we drove to the building where our meeting was going forward and had a delightful time. We then met with Henry Burkhardt, our president of the Dresden Mission. The meeting was held in our automobile so that no listening devices could record our conversation.

It was a privilege to meet with this giant of the Lord

who goes forward in directing our affairs behind the Iron Curtain without regard to any consequence to himself or his family. I conveyed to Brother Burkhardt personal greetings of the General Authorities of the Church, including the personal message from President Harold B. Lee, who said, "Tell Brother Burkhardt that he and his associates, while absent from our presence, are never absent from our prayers and our thoughts. We commend them for their spirituality; we sustain them in their important responsibilities." Brother Burkhardt was touched emotionally by this greeting.

The inspiration came to me to ask Brother Burkhardt a question. I said, through an interpreter, "Brother Burkhardt, do you think that if the invitation to come to general conference were sent to your government authorities, phrased in the correct way, they might give you such an opportunity?"

Brother Burkhardt is a man of great faith. He responded, "I believe the Lord will open the way." I shall surely pursue this matter.

As Brother Burkhardt walked from our car out into the rainy night, I could not help but realize that the day of sacrifice is not over and that there serve in the Church today men equally as dynamic and spiritually powerful as in any dispensation.

SUNDAY, OCTOBER 25, 1970

Met in district conference with the Erfurt District of the Dresden Mission. In the Dresden Mission are approximately forty-seven hundred members, situated in forty-seven branches in seven districts, Erfurt being one of these districts. One hundred and twenty-five were present at our

Priesthood leaders of the Dresden Mission rejoice in the brotherhood of the gospel as they gather for a conference in 1970.

district conference. The singing was outstanding, the spirit beautiful, and the friendship beyond description.

At the conclusion of the meeting I greeted each person there with a firm handclasp and the assurance that our Heavenly Father was mindful of his or her devotion and that indeed we are brothers and sisters in the gospel.

Following the conference, President and Sister Bryson and I returned to Berlin; and after once again passing by the many border guards, we went to the Schweizerhof Hotel, where we stayed the evening.

A few statistics pertaining to the Dresden Mission:

• There is a backlog of eight hundred worthy persons requesting patriarchal blessings.

• Two chapels are ready for dedication—one at Neubrandenburg and one in the Annaberg-Bucholtz area.

• Attendance figures for the month of August 1970 are as follows:

Sacrament meeting, 26 percent

Priesthood meeting, 35 percent

Primary, 50 percent

Relief Society, 35 percent

Sunday School, 65 percent

• In the mission there are six elders quorums.

• During the fiscal year 1969–70, there were nineteen convert baptisms, plus the baptisms of twenty-two children of record.

• More than three hundred youth participated in the youth conference during 1970. The closing song of the conference was "God Be with You Till We Meet Again." The opening song was one which has become a favorite, "If the Way Be Full of Trial, Weary Not."

MONDAY, OCTOBER 26, 1970

Flew to Düsseldorf, Germany, where I met with President Walter H. Kindt of the Germany Central Mission.

Today I also met with the missionaries who serve in that mission, including Elder Marc Larson. This was most inspirational. Just two weeks ago I was scheduled to attend a conference of the Grand Junction Colorado Stake. As the plane circled the airport amidst heavy snow, the pilot's voice announced that it appeared our landing would not be possible, and Grand Junction would of necessity be overflown. I knew that I had been assigned to this conference by a prophet and prayed that the weather would permit a landing. Suddenly the pilot said, "There is an opening in the cover. We'll *attempt* a landing." (That phrase is always a bit frightening to an air traveler.)

Our landing was safely accomplished, and the entire conference went without incident. I wondered why I particularly had been assigned here. Before departing Grand Junction, the stake president asked if I would meet with a distraught mother and father whose son had announced his decision to leave his mission field after having just arrived there. When the conference throng had left, we knelt quietly in a private place—mother, father, stake president, and I. As I prayed in behalf of all, I could hear the muffled sobs of a sorrowing mother and disappointed father.

When we arose, the father said, "Brother Monson, do you really think our Heavenly Father can alter our son's announced decision to return home before completing his mission? Why is it that now when I am trying so hard to do what is right, my prayers are not heard?"

I responded, "Where is your son serving?"

He replied, "In Düsseldorf, Germany."

I placed my arm around the mother and father and said to them, "Your prayers have been heard and are already being answered. With more than twenty-eight stake conferences being held this day and attended by the General Authorities, I was assigned to your stake. Of all the Brethren, I am the only one who has the assignment to meet in just two weeks with the missionaries in the Germany Central Mission, which includes Düsseldorf."

I met with Elder Larson today, and he has responded to the pleading of his parents. He has made a commitment to remain and complete his mission.

THURSDAY, MARCH 30, 1972

Attended the regular meeting of the First Presidency and Council of the Twelve. This was the meeting attended by all General Authorities in preparation for the forthcoming annual conference. It was inspirational to participate in the sacrament service and likewise in the testimonies.

Following the meeting, Gordon B. Hinckley, Stanley D. Rees, Henry Burkhardt, and I participated in a meeting with the First Presidency, that Henry Burkhardt might provide a full report. Brother Burkhardt is the president of the Dresden Mission. It was my opportunity to ordain him a high priest and set him apart some time ago to preside over that mission, which comprises almost five thousand members of the Church behind the Iron Curtain. It was a glorious privilege to hear Brother Burkhardt report firsthand to the Presidency of the Church. This was a dream come true. Of course he had to leave his wife and children at home in East Germany as hostages, the Communist government not permitting them to travel as a family to a land of freedom. The First Presidency seemed very pleased with the report of progress provided by Brother Burkhardt.

WEDNESDAY, APRIL 5, 1972

In the evening, Frances and I participated in a dinner honoring Henry Burkhardt, held at the home of Stanley Rees, to which were invited many mission presidents who had served in Germany with their wives, as well as Percy K. Fetzer, Gordon B. Hinckley, and their wives.

SUNDAY, APRIL 9, 1972

In the late afternoon Gordon B. Hinckley and I went over to the Assembly Hall for the final portion of the German-speaking conference session, which was addressed by Henry Burkhardt. I bade a fond farewell to Henry and asked that he convey my love to his choice counselors and likewise his dear wife and family. I am grateful to the Lord for the miraculous way in which Henry Burkhardt was granted the privilege of attending conference.

WEDNESDAY, NOVEMBER 8, 1972

Had a delightful meeting this morning with Percy Fetzer, wherein we reviewed matters relating to East Germany.

WEDNESDAY, MARCH 28, 1973

Frances and I picked up Thelma Fetzer and joined Stanley and Helen Rees at the Salt Lake City airport in waiting for the arrival of the plane carrying Brother Walter Krause and his wife, Edith, from East Germany. Sister Krause's brother also was at the airport to meet his sister. He has been separated from her for some nineteen and a half years. I don't know when I have been more happy to see someone and more pleased with the intervention of the Lord in making such a visit possible than on this particular occasion. The only possible thing with which to compare it was the miraculous way in which Henry Burkhardt was permitted to come to our conference just one year ago.

TUESDAY, APRIL 3, 1973

Attended the regular Missionary Executive Committee meeting, after which Frances, Percy and Thelma Fetzer, Helen and Stanley Rees, and Edith and Walter Krause joined me for a meeting with the First Presidency. The purpose of the meeting was to permit President Harold B. Lee and his counselors to meet Brother and Sister Krause. The First Presidency was most impressed with the spirituality of this choice couple and gained a greater appreciation for the many hardships with which our Saints behind the Iron Curtain must contend as they pursue the work of the Lord.

To Brother and Sister Krause, I think meeting the prophet of God was the highlight of their visit to Salt Lake City, and indeed one of the most inspirational experiences of their lives.

President Lee advised Brother Krause that the First Presidency and the Twelve had considered the possibility of his being ordained a patriarch, that he might give blessings to his people in East Germany.

Following the meeting with the Presidency, we adjourned to my office, where President Spencer W. Kimball ordained Brother Krause to the office of patriarch. It was my opportunity to stand by Brother Kimball's side, along with Elder Theodore M. Burton, as President Kimball served as voice and Brother Burton translated the ordination. Now the five thousand members of the Church in East Germany will not be required to wait such a long period of time to obtain their blessings from Brother Percy Fetzer; Brother Krause can give the blessings as he travels throughout Communist countries.

THURSDAY, JUNE 28, 1973

Today I had a telephone call from Brother Francis M. Gibbons, secretary to the First Presidency. He told me about a couple from East Germany who were miraculously able to be here in Salt Lake City, who desired to go to the temple but had no temple recommends. Could I take it from there? So Brother and Sister Demonovsky, from a branch perhaps a hundred miles from East Berlin, came into my office. She spoke English; he spoke only German. As I visited with them I knew I needed help, so I called Brother Percy Fetzer, who was in the middle of a rather important meeting in his cabinet company. He immediately closed the meeting and was in my office within ten minutes. He served as the interpreter as we visited with these choice people.

Sister Demonovsky had been a Relief Society president in East Germany, and Brother Demonovsky had been the Sunday School president, and miracle of miracles, they had been able to join a tour, a private tour of business people, who had come to America. The East German government allowed the tour because all the participants were over the age of sixty-five, an age when the government no longer cares so much whether or not they will return to East Germany. The Demonovskys have a married daughter here in Salt Lake, active in the Church, who with all her heart had prayed that the day would come when she could be sealed to her mother and father. Brother and Sister Demonovsky had been sealed in the Swiss Temple in about 1956.

I conducted the interview, Brother Fetzer being the interpreter. I telephoned Brother Eugene Bryson in Hamburg and he gave them a fine recommendation, and then recommends to the temple were issued. The lovely daughter threw her arms around her mother and father and said that a prayer of a lifetime had been realized.

Brother Demonovsky took through the temple as proxy the name of a deceased son. This child was also sealed by proxy to his parents. Sister Demonovsky took the name of a deceased granddaughter as her assigned name as she went through the temple. I had telephoned Horace Beesley, and he dropped everything and accompanied them through the temple, serving as their interpreter. He also performed the sealing ordinances.

I marveled at how our Heavenly Father brings to pass

in a simple way the yearnings of the hearts of Latter-day Saints. Though Communism and Iron Curtains may separate, our Heavenly Father can bring together the persons whom He needs, and He does so in His own way.

SUNDAY, AUGUST 26, 1973

Today we are in Munich, West Germany, for an area conference. This morning the Tabernacle Choir sang at the conference. They truly rose to great heights. Likewise, from Munich, *Music and the Spoken Word* was presented to a worldwide audience.

In the afternoon session I had the privilege to speak, my subject being reflected in the title of my address, "A Quest for Peace."

President Lee spoke approximately an hour. During his remarks, he made this statement, which I consider to be significant: "The Brethren of the General Authorities cannot be expected to become proficient in every language spoken by members of the Church, but the members can all learn English. I would like to leave that as a challenge for you." Going well beyond the closing period, he literally lifted the people close to God. There wasn't a dry eye in the audience as he concluded and the choir sang the beautiful number, "God Be with You Till We Meet Again." It was a spiritual feast for all who attended.

One highlight of the conference for Frances and me was seeing Brother and Sister Gustav Wacker, our dear Canadian friends, in the congregation. Brother Wacker was originally from Germany. I thought back to the time I served as president of the Canadian Mission and Brother Wacker and his wife lived in the Kingston Branch, where he served as the branch president. He was a barber by trade. I had occasion to look at his tithing record, and the tithing he was paying was far more than a barber would earn. So I decided to talk to his wife about it. I said to her, "Sister Wacker, you speak a little better English than your husband. I note that your husband is paying substantial tithing."

She said, "Oh, yes, President Monson."

I said, "It is far more than 10 percent, I believe."

"Oh, yes," she said.

"Well, you are only required to pay 10 percent."

"Oh, I know," she said, "but my husband and I, we love to pay it."

I wasn't getting anywhere with Sister Wacker, so I talked with Brother Wacker. I said, "I think you are paying perhaps 40 percent of your income as tithing. Did you know that the Lord requires only 10 percent?"

"Oh, *ya,* Brother Monson, *ya.* But perhaps the Lord needs my money elsewhere."

I said, "Brother Wacker, the Kingston Branch is meeting in a rented hall. We need a chapel in Kingston. Why don't you put a little of the money in a chapel fund and let just 10 percent go to the Lord as tithing?"

He said, "Oh, Brother Monson, there may be other people in other parts of the world who need a building more than we do. I will keep sending it to Church headquarters."

Brother Wacker never owned a car. He would cut the hair of the missionaries, and when they would attempt to pay him, he would always say to them, "I cannot take your money. It is a pleasure to cut the hair of a servant of the Lord." If it had been raining, he would reach into his pockets and give the missionaries any tips that he had earned that day. "Take a taxi home," he would say to them, "so you don't get wet or catch a cold." Then he would bundle his coat up around his ears and walk home in the rain.

It was always a privilege to be in the presence of Gustav and Marguerite Wacker. They are absolutely dedicated to the work of the Lord. Brother and Sister Wacker are now on a mission in Germany. As I sat in the mammoth building in which our conference was held, formerly an Olympic event building, and looked over perhaps twenty-three thousand members from all over Europe who had come for this conference, I said to Frances, "I wonder if Brother and Sister Wacker are somewhere in this gigantic auditorium. I would surely love to see them." With this thought in mind, we left the stand after the meeting and walked up the staircase to the area which would lead to the exit. I felt someone tugging on my coat. I turned around, and there were our dear and cherished friends Brother and Sister Wacker, sitting right next to the aisle—the only aisle that I could have exited and had the opportunity to greet them. I embraced them, and they shed tears. I shed tears. I knew the Lord had answered my prayer.

I held a meeting at the conference with the presidency of the Dresden Mission—President Burkhardt and his counselors. They had been allowed by the East German government to come to the conference. Also, besides these three brethren, six or seven district presidents were present along with approximately two hundred elderly people from behind the Iron Curtain. Our young, aggressive leaders were not permitted by the government to bring their wives.

It was a joy to watch the expression on the face of Walter Krause, our newly ordained patriarch for the Dresden Mission, as he listened with rapt attention to the conference and particularly the music by the Tabernacle Choir.

We had pledged to the East German government that all those who were permitted to attend would return. One elderly woman passed away, but true to our word, we made certain that her body was returned to East Germany.

All in all, fine tribute is due Elders J. Thomas Fyans, F. Enzio Busche, and Jacob de Jager for a superb coordination assignment. Our son Tom came to the conference following the completion of his mission in Milan, Italy. He felt that Brother de Jager's talk was a classic, as did we. Elder de Jager is very close to our family. My thoughts returned to the time when I presided over the Canadian Mission and Brother and Sister de Jager were baptized.

One Sunday during our mission, Frances was the only person in a usually very busy mission home. The telephone rang, and the person who was on the other end of the line spoke with a Dutch accent and asked, "Is this the headquarters of the Mormon Church?"

Frances assured him that it was, as far as Toronto was concerned. Then she asked, "May I help you?"

The party on the other end said, "Yes, we have come from our native Holland, where we have had an opportunity to learn something about the Mormons, and we would like to know a little more."

Frances responded, "I'm sure we can help you."

Then the caller said, "Would you wait just a little while, however, because we have chicken pox in our home. If you could wait until the children are well, we would love to have the missionaries call."

Frances indicated that she would arrange such and ended the conversation. Excitedly she told the two missionaries on our staff, "Here is a golden referral," and the missionaries responded excitedly. But, like some missionaries, they decided to procrastinate calling upon the family. Days turned into weeks, and the weeks became several. Finally Frances said, "Elders, are you going to call on that Dutch family?"

They responded, "We're too busy tonight, but we're going to get around to it."

A few more days went by. Again Frances asked, "What about my Dutch family? Are you going to call on them tonight?"

Again came the reply, "We're too busy tonight, but we're going to work it into our schedule."

Finally, they had crowded Frances too much, and she said, "If you aren't going to call on the Dutch family tonight, my husband and I will call on them."

They said, "We'll work it into our schedule tonight."

They called on this lovely family. They taught them the gospel. Each member of the family became a member of the Church. The family, of course, was the Jacob de Jager family. Brother de Jager became the president of our elders quorum. He worked with the gigantic Phillips Electronics Industries. He had worked in Mexico. He later became the counselor to several mission presidents in Holland, including Brother Max Pinegar. He became a Regional Representative of the Twelve, then became a member of the First Quorum of the Seventy.

In the evening we flew to London, there to remain the evening and catch our return flight home on Monday morning. We arrived in London almost two hours late, due to a flight controller slowdown in Germany.

3

"The Dawning of a New Beginning"

**REDEDICATION AND NEW HOPE
1974–77**

Attended the Leadership Committee meeting held in my office and other meetings throughout the day. One of my appointments was with Percy K. Fetzer and William T. South. We talked about the situation of the Church members in Czechoslovakia and determined to bring forth a recommendation that the Czech Saints comprise a district under the direction of the Dresden Mission. We felt inspired in this decision.

TUESDAY, APRIL 2, 1974

In the afternoon I met with President Spencer W. Kimball and introduced to him Brother and Sister Gottfried Richter, Brother Richter being the second counselor in the Dresden Mission, situated behind the Iron Curtain. We had a most enjoyable time with President Kimball. He spoke a little German and traced the Germanic ancestry of his wife's father and grandfather, all to the great delight of the Richters. Brother Stanley Rees, former president of the Germany North Mission, served as our interpreter.

Following this visit we went to the office of President N. Eldon Tanner. Brother John K. Fetzer served as our interpreter here. Sister Richter, a truly delightful person, was seated in the special chair which President Tanner has, which formerly was one of the council meeting chairs in the temple. When he told her that every apostle since Wilford Woodruff had sat on that particular chair, she beamed a smile of approval and obviously felt very privileged to be sitting there.

While we were visiting President Tanner, President Marion G. Romney came into the room, and the Richters had an opportunity to visit with him. I commented to the Brethren that Brother Richter is in private business as a stationer, and that through his good offices, he is able to provide the carbon paper without which we could not produce the materials which we use in our Church program in East Germany. A very restrictive law prevails there which prohibits printing of any kind for church organizations. The only way we can prepare resource material is to type an original and three carbon copies of every lesson a total of twelve times, which provides the forty-eight copies needed.

THURSDAY, MARCH 27, 1975

This evening I went to the Salt Lake City airport, where I joined Percy and Thelma Fetzer and others to await the arrival of Henry and Inge Burkhardt from Dresden, Germany. Of particular interest was the fact that earlier the governmental authorities had refused to grant Inge a visa. She had been downcast and so disappointed. The mission president, Gary Schwendiman, in Hamburg, Germany, had telephoned me and asked if we would place Inge Burkhardt's name on our prayer roll, that our Heavenly

March 1975: We greet the Burkhardts as they arrive at Salt Lake International Airport. Foreground, left to right: Inge Burkhardt, Henry Burkhardt, Percy K. Fetzer, and Elder Thomas S. Monson.

Father hopefully might intervene and arrange for her visa to be granted. This we did. Several days later when Brother Burkhardt went to the government officials, they granted the visa with no reference to their previous denial of the same. Surely our Heavenly Father responds to the faith of His people.

SATURDAY, APRIL 5, 1975

Late this afternoon I met with Howard W. Hunter and others, including Church Financial Department representative Alan Blodgett, so that Howard W. Hunter, Bruce R. McConkie, and others would understand all aspects of the financial situation in the Dresden Mission, inasmuch as its responsibility will now pass from me to the Missionary Executive Committee, chaired by Elders Hunter and McConkie.

SATURDAY, APRIL 12, 1975

Attended the quarterly conference of the Taylorsville Utah Central Stake. I had previously asked for the privilege to have Elder Joseph B. Wirthlin, newly sustained Assistant to the Twelve, accompany me to the conference. In addition, Henry Burkhardt and Percy K. Fetzer attended as observers. The Taylorsville Utah Central Stake is an excellent stake, a good one for Brother Wirthlin and Brother Burkhardt to see in action.

SUNDAY, APRIL 13, 1975

This morning Brother and Sister Joseph B. Wirthlin picked Frances and me up, and we drove to the Taylorsville Utah Central Stake for the Sunday session of this stake conference. There we met President and Sister Percy K. Fetzer and President and Sister Henry Burkhardt. The stake presidency had provided beautiful orchid corsages for each of the sisters.

We had a pleasant time at the conference. I am impressed with Brother Wirthlin and his guileless and humble spirit. The congregation seemed to enjoy so much hearing from Brother and Sister Burkhardt. Brother and Sister Fetzer served as their interpreters.

FRIDAY, APRIL 25, 1975

Today I flew to Berlin by way of Frankfurt and was there met by President and Sister Gary Schwendiman of the Germany Hamburg Mission. We drove through Checkpoint

Charlie and into East Berlin and thence to the Dresden Mission, where that evening we held a lengthy mission presidency meeting with the presidency of the Dresden Mission: President Henry Burkhardt, President Walter Krause, and President Gottfried Richter. I mentioned to the brethren that while I was dedicating the land of Portugal earlier this week, I felt impressed that I should offer a similar prayer to invoke our Heavenly Father's blessings upon the German Democratic Republic. President Burkhardt was assigned to suggest a place where the dedicatory prayer could be offered, perhaps on Sunday morning.

SATURDAY, APRIL 26, 1975

Today was a very busy day wherein I held conference sessions for the Saints in the German Democratic Republic. At 11:00 A.M. we met with all of the priesthood leaders of the entire mission area. These brethren are eager to learn and were a most enthusiastic audience. At 1:00 P.M. there was convened a general session for all of the members in the northern part of the mission, there being perhaps 720 in attendance.

Following this session, we returned to the hotel for a brief rest and then at 7:00 P.M. held a general leadership meeting for the group that had come from the southern part of the mission. I had no intention to deliver the message which the Lord prompted me subsequently to present. I had in mind discussing leadership principles, but I felt a strong and distinct impression to instead provide the leaders assembled personal glimpses into the life of each member of the First Presidency and Council of the Twelve. They seemed extremely pleased to receive this rather intimate

33

message concerning Brethren whom they revere, many of whom they have never seen in person.

Earlier in the day we visited the charred yet partially restored buildings of the Dresden area and again reflected upon the fire bombing during World War II in which British and American air forces destroyed the city, killing many thousands in the process.

SUNDAY, APRIL 27, 1975

Last evening we had dinner at the hotel adjacent to the one where we stayed. It is rather disconcerting to have as the table guests next to you officers of the Russian Army, although conditions have noticeably improved in the German Democratic Republic since I first visited the area several years ago.

At 7:30 A.M., by appointment, the Dresden Mission presidency and their wives, President Schwendiman and his wife, and I left the hotel en route to Friedensburg, the location which had been selected for the special prayer which I felt prompted to offer in this land. The setting was as beautiful a spot as could be imagined. We walked through the woods for about twenty minutes into a clearing overlooking the Elbe River, with Meissen on the right and Dresden on the left, Meissen being the birthplace of Karl G. Maeser, the founder of Brigham Young University.

As I explained the purpose of the prayer, the Burkhardts, Krauses, and Richters particularly showed keen interest. During the prayer, I said, "May today mark the dawning of a new beginning of thy work in this land." As I spoke these words, we heard the unmistakable sound of a rooster crowing, followed by the pealing of a cathedral bell in the distance. The day had been overcast, but during the prayer the sun shone brilliantly upon us, warming our bodies and giving us the assurance that our Heavenly Father was pleased with the prayer which was being offered.

Following is the text of the prayer of rededication:

Our beloved Heavenly Father, under the inspiration of Thy Holy Spirit, which we acknowledge freely and appreciate greatly, we assemble on this mountainside on this, Thy holy day, to dedicate and rededicate this land for the advancement of the work of The Church of Jesus Christ of Latter-day Saints.

Thou knowest the faith of the people of this land—the many tens of thousands who have embraced Thy gospel and have served to build up Thy church wherever they have been. Thou knowest the sermons which they have preached in song, for they sing with their hearts and echo the feelings of their souls.

Thou knowest, Heavenly Father, the sufferings of this people, and Thou hast been near to them in times of trouble and in times of joy.

We express our gratitude unto Thee for the privilege we have of holding meetings here, for bringing to the membership of the Dresden Mission the entire program of the Church. These blessings were scarcely imaginable a few years ago. We confess before Thee that it has been through Thy intervention that this blessing has been brought to pass. We acknowledge thy hand in every aspect of our lives and pledge our lives to Thy service.

In the authority of the holy apostleship which I bear, and in the name of Thy Beloved Son, Jesus Christ, the Savior and Redeemer of the world, I dedicate and rededicate this land for the advancement of Thy work.

I invoke, Heavenly Father, upon this people Thy divine blessings. Wilt Thou bless the membership of the Church. Grant that every member may have a desire to serve Thee and keep Thy commandments. Father, we ask Thee to cause that each one who is called to serve may serve with all of his heart and all of his strength. Grant unto Thy membership here a significant blessing, the blessing mentioned in the book of Third John: "I have no greater joy than to hear that my children walk in truth" (3 Jn. 1:4). Grant that the children of the membership of the Church in the Dresden Mission may be loyal to Thy cause, and the grandchildren, even unto the last generation before the second coming of Thy Beloved Son. Grant, Heavenly Father, that the membership here may receive their patriarchal blessings and live in such a way as to bring the promises to fulfillment.

Heavenly Father, wilt Thou open up the way that the faithful may be accorded the privilege of going to Thy holy temple, there to receive their holy endowments and to be sealed as families for time and all eternity.

Heavenly Father, we invoke a blessing upon the non-members of this land, that they may be touched in their hearts, that they may respond to the examples which the members set before them. Arouse within them a curiosity concerning the Church, and then cause that this curiosity may turn to a desire to know more, and then that this desire to know more will result in conversion to the gospel and that the membership of the Church may stabilize and indeed grow.

Heavenly Father, wilt Thou intervene in the governmental affairs. Cause that Thy Holy Spirit may dwell with those who preside, that their hearts may be touched and that they may make those decisions which would help in the advancement of Thy work.

We seek a blessing of peace upon this people, the peace promised by Thy Beloved Son. We look forward to the day when Thy missionaries may again be permitted to preach the everlasting gospel in this area, for we know there is much of the blood of Israel here. May today mark the dawning of a new beginning of thy work in this land.

Amidst the ringing of church bells this morning and the singing of birds in this, the forest which Thou hast created, music fills our souls and gratitude fills our hearts as we humbly acknowledge before Thee that Thou art our Father, that with Thee all things are possible, and that Thy gospel has been restored upon the earth.

Let the word go forth from this place, Heavenly Father. In Thy due time grant that many hundreds may seek membership in Thy church, and that Thy children whom Thou hast preserved may indeed be saved in the celestial kingdom of God.

Our Heavenly Father, wilt Thou bless the president of the Dresden Mission. We know of no man of greater faith in Thy kingdom. And for a man to serve as he has served has required the support of a devoted companion.

Bless the counselors in the mission presidency who stand by the side of the president and perform a marvelous work and a wonder among this people. Bless their companions and the families of each member of the presidency. Grant unto these men Thy power, for they are men who are righteous in the use of power and who are resolute and true in defending Thy word.

Shower down upon us, Heavenly Father, Thy bounteous blessings. Bring to this land Zion in all of its glory. Bring to the heart of each member a firm testimony of the gospel and grant that from this day forth, the way may be opened for Thy word to go forward in greater power. Grant that the way may be cleared for the program of the Church in its fulness to come to this people, for they, through their faith, have merited such blessings.

As Thy humble servant, acknowledging the divine revelation and inspiration of this day, I therefore invoke Thy holy blessings upon Thy work and upon Thy people in the Dresden Mission of The Church of Jesus Christ of Latter-day Saints.

We as a group acknowledge before Thee our indebtedness to Thee and place in Thee our trust, knowing that Thou issued a holy promise. Thou hast said, "I, the Lord, am merciful and gracious unto those who fear me, and delight to honor those who serve me in righteousness and in truth unto the end. Great shall be their reward and eternal shall be their glory."

With these divine words from the seventy-sixth section of the Doctrine and Covenants ringing in our ears, we offer up unto Thee this dedication and rededication prayer, in the name of Thy Beloved Son, Jesus Christ, amen.

As we returned to our automobiles, the sun disappeared from the sky and the overcast condition which previously existed once again prevailed. I think I have not enjoyed a more spiritual experience as a member of the Council of the Twelve than the experience of offering the prayer in this Communist-controlled land, invoking the blessings of our Heavenly Father on as faithful a group of Saints as ever existed.

At 10:00 A.M. we held a general session for all of the membership in the greater Dresden area. Two unusual experiences occurred during the general session. I felt impressed to call upon a Sister Sabine Baasch, a young, blonde seventeen-year-old member who was singing in the chorus, to bear her testimony. I felt impressed to call upon her even though I knew that President Henry Burkhardt had been asked to call upon two young people, and I had no idea whom he had selected. To my surprise, the young lady whom he had selected was none other than Sister Baasch. After she bore her testimony, she rendered a beautiful solo, impromptu, "O My Father" (*Hymns*, no. 292). I told her that the Lord had called upon her to speak and bear her testimony in word and song that day. Of this I am certain. Her father was the leader of the chorus and is a professional musician from Leipzig.

At the conclusion of the meeting, the Saints sang, "God be with you till we meet again. Auf Wiedersehen, auf

Wiedersehen." Each person's eyes were filled with tears, and handkerchiefs were everywhere in view as I bade a tender farewell to these, the most wonderful Saints to be found anywhere.

As I walked from the pulpit, a lady came up to me and introduced herself and her young son, Reinhold Daniel Sommer, from Görlitz, a city near Dresden. She said that six years ago when I was in Görlitz, she had just lost a child, a son, and appealed to me for consolation. I told her that if she were faithful, our Heavenly Father would bless her with another son. She mentioned that almost exactly nine months later, Reinhold Daniel was born and that he was the answer to that particular promise and prayer.

We chatted informally in the mission office, and then it was my opportunity to bless a choice couple. Benno Kurt Meyer had suffered a stroke and was making progress toward his recovery. Following the blessing which I provided Brother Meyer, I laid my hands upon the head of Hildegaard Lizbeth Meyer. As I began to bless her, I felt impressed to tell her that the loving service she had rendered her husband in his illness had been recorded in heaven and that our Heavenly Father would bless her abundantly for her kindness. As I continued in the blessing, brilliant sunlight came through the window and enveloped us. I felt this was a prompting of our Heavenly Father and felt impressed to promise Sister Meyer that her hip operation would be a success and that the doctors would be inspired of God and that her recovery would be complete. Rare are the occasions when one feels such a strong influence of the Spirit as was the case today.

In the late afternoon we returned to Berlin, where I spoke to approximately 250, including servicemen and their families, and many missionaries. A microphone had not been provided, so I had to strain my voice in speaking. I was coming down with a cold anyway, so this experience did not help matters.

Following the meeting, I visited with Elder Richard Plew, a young man who formerly dated our daughter, Ann, and who is a brother to Carol Scott, a dear friend of ours. Steve Scott, Carol's husband, who is also a dear friend, is a member of our bishopric.

We stayed at the Schweizerhof Hotel and had dinner with Brother and Sister Gordon Mortensen of the Berlin Stake presidency. We also had an opportunity to visit with President Dieter Berndt, whom I consider one of the strongest German leaders in Berlin, and Sister Berndt.

MONDAY, APRIL 28, 1975

This morning I flew from Berlin to Hamburg and thence to Amsterdam, where I was met at the airport by President and Sister Neil Kooyman of the Netherlands Mission.

TUESDAY, OCTOBER 7, 1975

Met today with Elder Joseph Wirthlin prior to his departure for Frankfurt, Germany. I am impressed that Brother Wirthlin is a man of great devotion and dogged determination. He will make a very able mission supervisor.

WEDNESDAY, OCTOBER 15, 1975

Met this morning with David Kennedy, special ambassador of the First Presidency. We discussed how best to proceed in East Germany, Czechoslovakia, and Poland with matters pertaining to our Church organization. Brother Kennedy agreed that the Dresden Mission should continue to supervise work in Czechoslovakia and Poland and that the Dresden Mission itself should continue under the direction of the Hamburg Germany Mission. I fully agree with this observation.

TUESDAY, NOVEMBER 18, 1975

This evening Frances and I went to the home of Percy and Thelma Fetzer, where we met with Stan and Helen Rees, Gene and Grace Bryson, and others in a special party honoring the mother of Henry Burkhardt. She is visiting from East Germany. Of interest was the fact that this was her first reunion with her brothers, Kurt and Otto Hunger, from whom she has been separated for over forty-five years.

TUESDAY, APRIL 13, 1976

This evening Frances and I attended an open house at the home of Percy and Thelma Fetzer, held in honor of Walter and Edith Krause of East Germany, who came for general conference and who will soon be returning to their home. Brother Krause is the patriarch in that area and gives blessings to worthy members behind the Iron Curtain. These are wonderful people, and we were pleased to be with them once again.

TUESDAY, MARCH 29, 1977

In the evening, we attended an open house at the home of Gary and Marva Schwendiman, honoring Henry Burkhardt and his wife, Inge. They are here to attend the general conference.

FRIDAY, APRIL 1, 1977

Today I, with the other Brethren, attended a day-long seminar for Regional Representatives of the Twelve. The wives of the Regional Representatives had also been invited to accompany their husbands to the meetings. The highlight was the afternoon testimony meeting held in the Assembly Room of the Salt Lake Temple. I slipped a note to President N. Eldon Tanner, who was conducting the meeting, suggesting that perhaps Henry Burkhardt could be called upon. Not only was Henry given this privilege, but his wife, Inge, as well. As Gary Schwendiman translated for each one of them, I noticed many handkerchiefs wiping moist eyes throughout the congregation. It was thrilling to see these choice people in attendance in this special room.

4

"They Sing with Their Hearts"

**BLESSINGS, PROGRESS,
AND INSPIRATION
1978–79**

SATURDAY, MARCH 4, 1978

Frances and I flew to Berlin by way of Frankfurt, and after a moment of refreshment at the Schweizerhof Hotel in Berlin, we went across Checkpoint Charlie into East Berlin. Here we almost missed making contact with the Burkhardts. Since our planes had been delayed in arriving and arrangements had not been foolproof, Brothers Burkhardt and Richter had returned to the hotel. Brother Schulze, the second counselor, was the last one to leave the meeting, and by what to some would seem chance, he happened to recognize us in the rented cars we were driving. He stopped and advised us where we could rendezvous at the hotel. Had we not seen him, the entire visit would have been in vain, for we would have assumed that the Dresden Mission presidency had returned to Dresden. As it was, the sisters went to the opera and we participated in a lengthy administrative meeting relative to the future of the Dresden Mission. Those participating in the meeting were Elder Joseph B. Wirthlin, Regional Representative Dan Jorgensen, Henry Burkhardt, Brother Richter, Brother Schulze, and I.

SUNDAY, MARCH 5, 1978

Flew from Berlin to Frankfurt, staying at the home of Brother and Sister Wirthlin.

WEDNESDAY, MARCH 29, 1978

Held a full discussion this morning relative to the Dresden Mission and how we might best serve our members in that part of Germany. In attendance were Theodore Burton, Joseph Wirthlin, Neal Maxwell, Gottfried Richter, Gary Schwendiman, Victor Brown, and I. We all recognize that the Dresden Mission is different from any ecclesiastical unit in the Church and has to be approached keeping this fact in mind.

WEDNESDAY, APRIL 5, 1978

Met with the First Presidency this morning, accompanied by Neal Maxwell and James Faust, and presented my plan for the Dresden Mission. It consisted pretty much of carrying on as we are at present but with some effort toward amalgamation of two small districts—Zwickau and Karl-Marx-Stadt—and the provision of additional leadership opportunities, both here and in Dresden, for the mission leaders as well as district and branch leaders in Dresden itself. The First Presidency seemed to look with favor on the presentation and asked that I repeat it in the meeting of the First Presidency and the Twelve. They indicated they would like me to carry on as a liaison with this delicate area of the world.

THURSDAY, APRIL 6, 1978

During our regular temple meeting today, I presented my formal recommendations relating to the Dresden

Mission. The Brethren seemed to respond favorably to the recommendations. Elder Mark E. Petersen asked if I had any reluctance about crossing the border into East Germany. I told him, "Absolutely not!" He made the motion that I continue my assignment there. There were many who seconded the motion. They then recommended that I make a visit to that area at least once a year. The First Presidency concurred.

FRIDAY, APRIL 28, 1978

This morning we flew to Frankfurt and thence to Berlin, where we were met by Elder Charles Didier, his wife, Lucie, and Dan Jorgensen. We then entered Checkpoint Charlie and crossed the border into East Berlin.

At our rendezvous point with Henry Burkhardt and his counselors, we were advised by Henry that our former meeting in East Berlin had been monitored by government agencies and that it would be unsafe for us to convene our session at our own meetinghouse.

We met at the apartment of members, which was situated above a small bakery operated by the family. We had a lovely time and a choice meeting wherein we accomplished the instructions to Brother Burkhardt and his counselors relating to the decisions which the First Presidency and the Council of the Twelve had made concerning the work in the Dresden Mission.

Such items included the combination of the Zwickau and Karl-Marx-Stadt Districts; the visiting plan of General Authorities and board members from headquarters; separation of the temporal and ecclesiastical side of Brother Burkhardt's work, with one phase coming under the direction of Regional Representative Dan Jorgensen and Elder Theodore Burton, area supervisor, and with the other phase

45

coming under the direction of John Creer, the Presiding Bishopric's area supervisor situated in Frankfurt. Other aspects of the work were also discussed and decisions made.

I felt impressed to give a blessing to the owner of the bakery, Brother Wilhelm Brüning. He had been suffering from diabetes and had recently had surgery on his foot which had been most painful to him. After this blessing, I was impressed to offer a blessing upon the home and upon the family. In attendance were the father and mother, a sixteen-year-old daughter, and nine-year-old son. A lovely spirit prevailed. I cannot help but feel that our Heavenly Father will reward the devotion of such choice members of the Church who live and who worship under such difficult circumstances.

Following our meeting, Frances and I returned to West Berlin, and Charles and Lucie Didier proceeded on to Dresden for the conference there. Dan Jorgensen returned with us. Elder Delbert L. Stapley has been gravely ill; hence, it was felt best that I be available to a telephone rather than in a Communist country, in the event he should pass away and the Twelve would need to be notified.

WEDNESDAY, MAY 24, 1978

This afternoon I met with Robert and Shirley Thomas, Sister Thomas being a counselor in the General Relief Society presidency, and Brother and Sister Shumway, to prepare them for their visit to the Dresden Mission. Naomi Shumway is the general president of the Primary Association. I believe these individuals will perform admirably in providing leadership help to our Saints in the Dresden Mission. I think back to the day when I asked Henry Burkhardt whether he felt it would be possible for us to bring the program to the Saints since the Saints could not leave East Germany to receive the program elsewhere. His answer: "Let us give it a try." The Lord has surely opened the way for such to be accomplished.

THURSDAY, MAY 25, 1978

Attended the regular temple meeting, after which President Kimball asked that I remain and meet with him and his counselors relative to a discussion pertaining to our Saints in East Germany and the inability of the Saints to receive temple ordinances. It was a very profitable discussion.

FRIDAY, AUGUST 25, 1978

After a lengthy delay in London, due to airline connections and an air controllers' strike over France, I arrived at 6:00 P.M. at Tegel Airport in Berlin. Regional Representative Dan Jorgensen and I crossed the checkpoint and met at a prearranged meeting place in East Berlin with Henry Burkhardt and his counselor, President Gunther Schulze. We reviewed in detail the matter of the inability of our Saints in East Germany to receive their endowments at the temple. We discussed a plan whereby six specified couples' names would be provided to David Kennedy, and he in turn would make an effort with the government to emphasize the importance of a one-time visit to the temple by every Latter-day Saint. The theory was that if we could establish a record of credibility, with about six couples going to the temple for their own endowments and sealings and returning to their homes in the German Democratic Republic, and then having perhaps six other couples go, the approximately eight hundred worthy but unendowed persons in the German Democratic Republic could receive these blessings. Alternate methods were also discussed.

In the late evening we returned to the checkpoint and to the Schweizerhof Hotel in Berlin. One never ceases to marvel at the faith and devotion of such men as Brothers Burkhardt and Schulze. We are very fortunate indeed to have them in positions of responsibility, directing our approximately forty-two hundred members in that nation.

FRIDAY, SEPTEMBER 8, 1978

Held a meeting with the First Presidency relative to East Germany and the visit of David Kennedy to that country. Our desire is to open up a way for faithful members of the Church in that land to gain exit visas to have their sacred ordinances performed in the Swiss Temple, after which they would return to their homeland. Our hopes are high, but realistically, we feel our prospects for gaining the necessary approval are rather dim.

WEDNESDAY, SEPTEMBER 27, 1978

Attended a full day of meetings at the office. The highlight of the day was the opportunity to perform the sealing ceremony for Brother and Sister Gunther Schulze of the German Democratic Republic. Earlier in the year I had met with Brother and Sister Schulze in a car in a parking lot one rainy evening in East Germany. We met in the car to avoid the ever-present and everywhere-to-be-found government informers. Brother and Sister Schulze were third-generation members of the Church. I felt impressed to ask them if they had ever been to the house of the Lord. They replied that they hadn't but this was one of their great desires.

"Would it be possible, if a letter of invitation were sent, that your government would permit you to travel to the United States to visit one of the temples of God?" I asked.

"No, no," they replied. "Our position is too sensitive here." I could see great tears welling up in their eyes.

We bade one another farewell that evening, and they had walked only about ten paces away from me when I felt impressed to speak to them, using the little German I know. *"Bruder und Schwester Schulze, kommen Sie hier, bitte."* They returned and stood before me. Through an interpreter I said, "I feel that the Lord would like to see you endowed in His holy house. You are worthy people; you are exemplary in the conduct of your lives; you are faithful in the pursuit of your Church responsibilities. Let's trust in the Lord. Let's let our faith exceed our doubt." I quoted that phrase from Stephen L Richards, "Faith and doubt cannot exist in the mind at the same time, for one will dispel the other." We knelt in the parking lot in the rain and poured out our hearts to God.

When I returned to Salt Lake City, we remembered both Brother and Sister Schulze on the prayer roll of the First Presidency and Council of the Twelve; and when we advised the government that we would like him to come to our general conference in Salt Lake City, permission was granted.

Today, therefore, was a day of fulfillment.

WEDNESDAY, OCTOBER 4, 1978

Immediately following the Church Coordinating Council session, it was my opportunity to invite Brother and Sister Gunther Schulze from the Dresden Mission to meet with the First Presidency. It was an experience the Schulzes will never forget.

FRIDAY, OCTOBER 20, 1978

Flew to Berlin and spent the afternoon visiting about the city. We welcomed Dan and Elaine Jorgensen in the evening and prepared for our visit to East Germany.

SATURDAY, OCTOBER 21, 1978

Today we crossed Checkpoint Charlie, and after considerable difficulty with respect to our accommodation vouchers, we were permitted to gain entry into East Germany. We drove through the beautiful countryside on a sunlit day until we arrived at the city of Dresden. There we had the opportunity to meet in leadership session and in general session with all of the Saints in the northern portion of the Dresden Mission. Four hundred and thirty-six attended the general session.

We remained overnight at Dresden.

SUNDAY, OCTOBER 22, 1978

Met in a leadership session with the priesthood leaders of the Dresden Mission south area, followed by a general session where 695 were in attendance. Frances and I both participated in the many meetings. It was her first time to visit the Saints of the Dresden Mission, and I am very happy that she had this opportunity to do so. I always come away from the Dresden Mission uplifted and inspired with the faith and devotion of our members. I truly consider my assignment with this choice body of Saints to be one of my most cherished experiences as a member of the Council of the Twelve. I have complete faith and confidence in President Henry Burkhardt and his able counselors.

Before driving back to Berlin, we visited the small cemetery in Dresden. It was a dark night, and a cold rain had been falling throughout the entire day. We had come to visit the grave of a missionary who many years before had died while in the service of the Lord. A hushed silence shrouded the scene as we gathered about the grave. With a flashlight illuminating the headstone, I read the inscription:

JOSEPH A. OTT
Born: 12 December 1870, Virgin, Utah
Died: 10 January 1896, Dresden, Germany

Then the light revealed that this grave was unlike any other in the cemetery. The marble headstone had been polished; weeds such as those which covered other graves had been carefully removed, and in their place was an immaculately edged bit of lawn and some beautiful flowers that told of tender and loving care. I asked, "Who has made this grave so attractive?" My query was met by silence.

At last a twelve-year-old deacon, Tobias Burkhardt, son of President Henry Burkhardt, acknowledged that he had wanted to render this unheralded kindness and, without prompting from parents or leaders, had done so. He said that he just wanted to do something for a missionary who gave his life while in the service of the Lord. I thanked him.

We held a service at the cemetery and then retired to the location where I had earlier had the privilege to rededicate the land of East Germany. There we had a brief service with a mild rain descending. I recounted the experiences of the day the dedicatory prayer was offered

Young Tobias Burkhardt, a deacon, quietly cared for the gravesite of Elder Joseph A. Ott, a faithful full-time missionary who died during his service in Germany.

and told of the sun bursting forth from its hiding place behind the dense clouds. I mentioned that the crow of a rooster and the ringing of church bells had heralded a new day for our church in that area on the day the country was rededicated.

We then returned to West Berlin after a rather arduous drive.

WEDNESDAY, NOVEMBER 22, 1978

This morning I had the privilege to meet with the First Presidency, there to discuss with the Brethren how we might provide the blessings of the temple to our worthy Saints in East Germany. I mentioned to the Presidency that the East German government has asked why we do not build a temple in their country for all of the socialist countries of Europe. They, of course, use the word *socialist* to refer to the Communist Bloc nations.

It appears as though the government will not permit its citizens to have visas to go to the Swiss Temple; hence, the only possible way we can provide endowment and sealing blessings for the Saints would be through providing a facility of our own in that country.

WEDNESDAY JANUARY 24, 1979

This morning I again met with the First Presidency to discuss the Dresden Mission and how our people might best receive their temple blessings. Due to their inability to leave East Germany, it may be necessary to provide some facilities there for such ordinance work.

SATURDAY, FEBRUARY 10, 1979

Took the plane to Berlin, Germany, where I had the opportunity to join Dan Jorgensen and Elder Theodore M. Burton. We had a special prayer at our hotel room, where I revealed to these brethren some tentative plans for a small facility to be erected in the German Democratic Republic for the purpose of temple work.

We then placed the temple drawings as inconspicuously as we could within Brother Jorgensen's briefcase and drove across the border into East Germany. There we met Henry

Burkhardt and, by prearrangement, stayed at the home of one of our members, the family having vacated for the weekend.

Henry Burkhardt had tears come to his eyes when he saw the beautiful drawings of a projected building. He felt very good about the proposal and will respond to his government's invitation now, in that they had previously suggested that perhaps a temple could be built in that country, rather than our requesting permission for citizens of the German Democratic Republic to go to Switzerland.

In the evening we had dinner at the Schweizerhof Hotel and met briefly with President Dieter Berndt of the Berlin Stake and President Glen Roylance of the Germany Hamburg Mission.

SUNDAY, FEBRUARY 11, 1979

This morning I boarded the plane in Berlin, Germany, for the long flight back to Salt Lake City. The planes on which I flew experienced a series of mechanical problems which were most unusual. As I boarded the British Airways plane from Berlin to England, we were told that the water pipes had frozen in the rest rooms, and therefore, we would need to deplane and board another flight. On the second flight, we were advised that the cold weather had broken some seals in the front landing gear; hence, it was necessary to board a third plane. Upon arrival in England, I discovered that the Pan American flight to Los Angeles was delayed a full hour because of the need to replace three tires on the jumbo jet.

Upon arrival in Los Angeles, after an eleven-hour flight, the plane landed just before the Los Angeles Airport closed because of fog. The flight was sufficiently late that I could not board my flight to Salt Lake City. The plane was waiting at the gate but was loaded, and as it taxied away, I could envision staying overnight in Los Angeles; however, after considerable delay, we were driven to Burbank, California, to board the Western Airlines flight to Salt Lake City. There was an additional one-hour delay here because the landing staircase could not be retracted on the new Boeing 737 plane. I finally arrived at Salt Lake City a little after midnight, realizing that I had been on the plane since eight o'clock that morning, plus a nine-hour time differential between Berlin and Salt Lake City.

WEDNESDAY, MARCH 14, 1979

Frances and I drove to Provo, Utah, to Walter Stover Hall, one of the Helaman Halls dormitories which houses young female students. Walter Stover, an immigrant from Germany, has been one of the most consistent and beneficent contributors to Brigham Young University over a long period of time. Each year the young ladies pay tribute to him by having a little dinner in his honor. Brother Stover's daughter and three grandchildren were with him. After a brief social period at the hall itself, we went to the cafeteria and had a lovely dinner served to us. Brother Stover and I were the two speakers.

Brother Stover has been a true friend to the Saints in Germany, having directed much of the work in that country following the devastation of World War II. He recounted the ravages which affected the land and the people during this period and then beautifully told the story of how the Dutch Saints had been asked, in the spring of 1947, to begin a welfare project of their own after they had received much-needed welfare supplies from the members in America. The

Walter Stover lived a life of generous service.

proposal was welcomed with enthusiasm. The priesthood went to work, and within a short time every quorum had found a suitable piece of land for the project. The recommended crop: potatoes. At the various branches of the Church there was singing, speaking, and praying, at the end of which the potatoes were entrusted to the soil. Soon there came news of good prospects for the harvest, and cautious estimates were made as to how large the yield would be.

During the time the potatoes were growing, Walter Stover visited the Netherlands Mission in Holland. During his visit, with tears in his eyes, he told of the hunger of the Church members in Germany. They were in worse condition than the Saints in the Netherlands. Supplies had not reached the Saints in Germany as quickly as they had the Saints in Holland.

When Cornelius Zappey, the Netherlands Mission president, heard of the condition of the German Saints, he couldn't help but have compassion toward them, knowing how they had suffered. The thought came, and the action followed: "Let's give our potatoes to the members of the Church in Germany." I'm sure he worried, for the German armies and the Dutch armies had been in conflict with each other. The Dutch had been starving. Would they respond?

At long last the day of harvest arrived. A Dutch widow who had received a sack of the potatoes heard that the bulk of the potatoes was to be given to the members in Germany, and she stepped forward and said, "My potatoes must be with them." And this hungry widow returned her sack of potatoes. The trucks were loaded, and the Dutch Saints headed for the German border, only to find that they were stopped because of a ban which precluded sending food-stuffs from Holland to other nations. President Zappey prayed for inspiration from the Lord and then told the border guards that these potatoes were consecrated potatoes in that they had been grown by the people in their gardens for a specific charitable purpose and that had this not been the purpose, there would have been no produce grown after this fashion. Fortunately, the guards were persuaded to his point of view, and the trucks proceeded on into Germany, where they were welcomed with thanksgiving and rejoicing.

Brother Stover also told the young ladies of the terrible conditions which existed following the Russian occupation of Germany. I do believe that his message and his sincerity

*The Berlin Dahlem Ward chapel is one of the buildings
donated to the Church by Walter Stover.*

conveyed a viewpoint and a feeling to the young women which they will long remember.

I think one of Brother Stover's most unusual accomplishments was hiring an entire train in Germany. Following the war, the Saints had no transportation, but Brother Stover had that train pick up the members of the Church all the way through the cities of Germany, that all could meet together as sons and daughters of God.

WEDNESDAY, MARCH 28, 1979

Met today with Henry and Inge Burkhardt, who are in Salt Lake City for general conference, along with President Gary Schwendiman, who served as their interpreter. It was wonderful to see Henry again and to have an update on the most important work he is accomplishing in the Dresden Mission.

Brother Burkhardt indicated that the government

authorities liked the building plans which we have submitted and, after indicating that Western money would be required to purchase materials, seemed to give the green light for us to proceed in our steps to have a suitable building in Karl-Marx-Stadt.

MONDAY, APRIL 2, 1979

Early this morning I held a meeting with Henry Burkhardt, Theodore Burton, Neal Maxwell, Joe Christensen, and others relating to the possibility of home seminary in the Dresden Mission. It appears that the materials could be simplified and reduced and become a course of study for adults, with young people becoming the secondary beneficiaries. Any program which is directed specifically to the youth is suspect in the German Democratic Republic.

WEDNESDAY, APRIL 11, 1979

Met early this morning with the First Presidency relative to matters in East Germany. Dan Jorgensen, Regional Representative, had prepared a position paper for Theodore Burton, and President Kimball had requested a copy of the same. This prompted President Kimball to desire further information regarding East Germany, which information I was able to supply.

TUESDAY, MAY 29, 1979

This afternoon I met with Brother Hans Schult from East Germany. I took Brother Schult in to meet President Spencer W. Kimball, which was no doubt the highlight of Brother Schult's life. He has been in Utah for perhaps fourteen days and has been to the temple for more than twenty sessions. I was much impressed with his spirit.

TUESDAY, OCTOBER 2, 1979

At 12:30 I had the privilege of performing the sealing ceremony for Brother and Sister Schult of the German Democratic Republic. He is the district president in East Berlin. Some time ago I asked the question, "Could a district president and his wife be invited to come to conference so that they might be endowed and sealed in the temple?" The answer: "Only if they go in lieu of a member of the Dresden Mission Presidency." Not wishing to give up any ground which we have earned with the government, I responded, "Let's see if we might submit a request for their permission in addition to a member of the Dresden Mission presidency." Such was granted.

I learned from Brother Schult a little background concerning this approval. He said that all of the religious leaders were called into a meeting in Dresden and asked how they might best honor the thirtieth anniversary of the founding of their country. The other religious leaders fawned over the government officials and waxed eloquent with praise. President Henry Burkhardt of the Dresden Mission called upon Gottfried Richter, his second counselor, to make a response in behalf of our church, whereupon Brother Richter quoted from the Doctrine and Covenants that governments were instituted for the blessing of people (see D&C 134:1). The government official was so interested in this direct revelation from God as contained in the Doctrine and Covenants that he indicated he was impressed. Some weeks later when Brother Schult, who was an engineer by trade, had his visa request denied by his local officials, the government officials in Dresden were asked to intercede, and as a result of the favorable impression made upon these officials in the anniversary ceremonies, one of the top leaders said, "It is in our best interest to allow Mr. Schult to go to America." We, of course, know that our Heavenly Father brought about the opportunity.

Later in the day I met with Theodore Burton and Gottfried Richter relative to matters in the German Democratic Republic and the building program which we are anxious to see move forward. The government has given tentative approval for our planned building in Karl-Marx-Stadt but indicated they are not ready to grant us permission to move forward yet.

At 3:30 in the afternoon I had the opportunity to visit with the son and daughter of Rudolph Cierpka, former president of our Berlin Germany Stake. Brother Cierpka was in Dresden as a medical officer at the time of the bombing near the end of World War II.

TUESDAY, NOVEMBER 6, 1979

I learned today that Sister Inge Burkhardt lies seriously ill in Dresden. She has undergone gallbladder surgery but has developed complications, including pneumonia. We are remembering her in our prayers.

FRIDAY, NOVEMBER 30, 1979

Departed this morning for a brief assignment to East Germany. I flew to New York City and caught the evening plane en route to Frankfurt, Germany.

SATURDAY, DECEMBER 1, 1979

Arrived in Frankfurt, Germany, early this morning and took the plane to Berlin. Although it was raining in Berlin and was a rather dismal day, I enjoyed walking through this beautiful city and awaited the arrival of Hans Ringger, a

Regional Representative from Zurich, and John Creer, our director for temporal affairs in Frankfurt.

In the evening we held a strategy meeting and enjoyed dinner together.

SUNDAY, DECEMBER 2, 1979

Early this morning we crossed the border into the German Democratic Republic. I was amazed at the ease with which Brother Ringger effected our entry. There is something particularly pleasing about the way a native Swiss is able to maneuver in international circles. We then rented a car and drove to Leipzig, where we met with the priesthood brethren and later with their families. The furnace in the Leipzig building had failed and repair parts were unobtainable; hence, the meeting was held in the cold.

There was no lack of warmth, however, in the hearts of the members. They had their scriptures with them, sang with gusto, and reflected a spirit of devotion to the gospel. I was told that of the thirty-nine elders in this branch, thirty-seven are active and were present in the building. How I wished I could speak German so I could communicate with these good people in their own language.

We then drove to a meeting point outside Dresden where we joined Brother and Sister Schultz and then journeyed to the hospital where Sister Inge Burkhardt is a patient. Sister Burkhardt, the wife of our mission president in the Dresden Mission, has had a difficult time since her gallbladder surgery, which was followed by complications such as pneumonia. She has been hospitalized for almost nine weeks. She was able to walk to a waiting room where we joined our faith and our prayers in providing her a blessing. I indicated to her that this blessing was the principal reason for my coming to East Germany. This thought seemed to touch all present in the room. A good spirit prevailed, and after a time of greeting, we also gave a blessing to Henry Burkhardt.

I shall never forget the scene as we departed from the hospital grounds, when looking upward we saw Sister Burkhardt from her bedroom window waving farewell to us. We journeyed without incident back to Berlin and stayed the night at the Schweizerhof Hotel. I was pleased, however, to bring with me a report from Henry Burkhardt that government authorities look with favor upon our erection of buildings in Leipzig and Karl-Marx-Stadt. The only problem seems to be the insufferable delays of government red tape.

MONDAY, DECEMBER 3, 1979

Departed Frankfurt en route to New York City, remaining in New York City in the evening.

5

"Bring to This Land Zion"

THE FIRST EAST GERMAN STAKE
1980–82

This afternoon I held a semiannual planning meeting relative to the German Democratic Republic and Dresden Mission. In attendance were Hans Ringger, Theodore Burton, Robert Hales, Henry Burkhardt, Gary Schwendiman, Burke Peterson, and I.

Frances and I attended sacrament meeting in the ward where our son, Tom, and his wife, Carma, live. They had a nice program arranged. At the conclusion, I was invited to speak and was happy to do so. I thanked key members of their ward for being so gracious to Brother and Sister Henry Burkhardt and Brother and Sister Schumann, who were here from East Germany. A Brother Lehnig, who is one of the clerks in Tom's ward, had a supervisory position in one of the dental labs in Salt Lake City. He was in the right place at the right time to assist Sister Burkhardt in supplying her with some dental work which she needed.

TUESDAY, MAY 27, 1980

Flew to Zurich, where I had a most productive meeting with President Percy K. Fetzer of the Swiss Temple and Hans Ringger, the Regional Representative for the Dresden Mission. We met at the Eden Au Lac and discussed in detail the matter of ordinance work for our people in the Dresden Mission.

President Fetzer told of a most inspirational ending to an experience which took place several years ago. At the time, he was serving as a patriarch, called to give blessings throughout the German-speaking portions of Europe. One day he was giving patriarchal blessings to a family by the name of Konietz in Selbongen, which was then part of Poland. The borders of the country were closed. As he placed his hands upon the head of each member, he pronounced some very unusual blessings. He promised a young son that he would serve a mission in another country. He promised a young daughter in the family that she would marry in the house of God. In the patriarchal blessings to the mother and father, he promised them they and the entire family would be together in a holy temple. None of these blessings appeared in the most remote way to be possible.

Brother Fetzer came into my office when he returned to the United States, and as he sat with me, he wept. He said, "Brother Monson, I have pronounced blessings which cannot be fulfilled, but I was persuaded by the Holy Spirit to say what I did. What shall I do?"

I said, "Brother Fetzer, you gave the blessings through the inspiration of our Heavenly Father, and with Him, all things are possible. Let's you and I kneel right now by the side of my desk and supplicate His help." As we arose from our knees, we knew that somehow the blessings would be fulfilled.

It was not long after that a treaty was negotiated with Poland, and all German nationals trapped at the end of the war in that country were permitted to come to the West. The Konietz family came to Dortmund. Brother Konietz became a bishop. Brother Fetzer reported today that the entire family had come to the temple in Switzerland to be sealed together for all eternity. The young boy who was promised he would serve a mission beyond his home has now been called, and the young daughter who was promised she would marry in the temple is now engaged and planning to be sealed in the Swiss Temple. Every promise of their patriarchal blessings is coming true. There came to my mind the expression, "The wisdom of God oft-times appears as foolishness to men, but the greatest single lesson we can learn in mortality is that when God speaks and a man obeys, that man will always be right."

SUNDAY, JUNE 29, 1980

Early this morning, Hans Ringger, our Regional Representative, and I crossed Checkpoint Charlie into East Germany, where we met with the presidency of the Germany Dresden Mission.

After our executive meeting, which was rather lengthy, we met with the Saints of the East Berlin District. What a joy to meet with these choice people. One little boy on the front row spent much of the meeting with a ballpoint pen, drawing a picture. He later presented the picture to me. It was a rather interesting reproduction of the Salt Lake Temple, with the various spires and the Angel Moroni prominently featured. The young lad had drawn the windows in the proper shapes, some being round and others of varying shapes. I thought it significant that this little boy, from the memory of a picture most probably shown him by his mother, had made a rendition of the temple which he may perhaps never see in his lifetime.

After all our meetings and business of the day had been transacted, we returned to West Berlin, where we were met by President Dieter Berndt of the Berlin Stake. We were taken to his home for a lovely dinner. We gave a blessing to Brother Berndt, in that his back is causing him difficulty. We also gave a blessing to Sister Berndt, who is in need of open-heart surgery and who has not enjoyed good health for several months. These are choice people.

TUESDAY, OCTOBER 14, 1980

After a full day of meetings, I had a session with Brother and Sister Gunther Schulze prior to their return to the Dresden Mission. Brother Schulze had had some physical distress while in Salt Lake City, so we provided him a full physical examination. We were very pleased with the outcome, for he has been provided adequate medicine, and the doctors feel confident that he will be all right.

THURSDAY, APRIL 2, 1981

Today was our temple meeting for all General Authorities prior to conference. After the expression of testimonies, we participated in a sacrament service and received counsel from the First Presidency.

In the afternoon I held my semiannual meeting with those who have responsibility pertaining to the Dresden Mission. All of us were disappointed that Sister Burkhardt was not granted permission to accompany her husband to this conference. We think it is a reaction of the government in the German Democratic Republic to the difficulties being experienced in Poland, which has become a focal point of sparring between the NATO forces and the Communist forces.

FRIDAY, APRIL 10, 1981

I met privately with Brother Henry Burkhardt, Gary Schwendiman being my interpreter. I am impressed with the worth of Brother Burkhardt to the building of the kingdom in the Dresden Mission. He is totally dedicated to the Lord and to his assignments.

WEDNESDAY, JUNE 3, 1981

In the afternoon the Deseret Management Corporation held its quarterly meeting, after which I met with Burke Peterson and Emil Fetzer relative to schematic plans for a new temple in the German Democratic Republic. It is a maze of bureaucracy to deal with the East German government. Any property would, of necessity, be on a long-term lease. We are hopeful that we can obtain a building for the purpose of providing our Saints with the privilege of receiving their endowments and participating in sealing ordinances. There is no other way which would offer so many blessings as would the provision of a small temple.

FRIDAY, JUNE 5, 1981

At 9:00 A.M. I met with the First Presidency and with Burke Peterson, there to discuss the matter of the proposed temple in the German Democratic Republic. I asked the brethren of the Presidency if they felt it was time to share with any of the other General Authorities the confidential work we are doing with regard to this building. The Presidency felt that such sharing could be deferred until we are more certain of our location and the approval of the plans of construction.

WEDNESDAY, SEPTEMBER 23, 1981

Today I met with others who have responsibility for the German Democratic Republic to discuss the proposed building in Freiberg. Things are progressing nicely, and it looks as though the public officials of the German Democratic Republic, due to their desire for hard Western currency, will be cooperative in the endeavor.

MONDAY, OCTOBER 12, 1981

One of the highlights of today was a meeting with Gottfried Richter and Sister Richter, who were here from the German Democratic Republic. Gary Schwendiman served as interpreter. How pleased I am that Brother and Sister Richter have been able to obtain their needed dental work. A Dr. James E. Russon contributed almost sixty hours of consecutive dentistry, setting aside his regular schedule. Brother Norbert Lehnig, a dental lab technician, did the same with respect to the service he rendered. I am pleased with the progress being made among the Church members in the Dresden Mission.

WEDNESDAY, DECEMBER 9, 1981

I had an opportunity to meet with a Sister Dietrich from East Germany. Gary Schwendiman served as our interpreter. Sister Dietrich had been suffering from a malfunctioning pacemaker. Through approval of her government, we were able to bring her to Salt Lake City, where Dr.

Russell Nelson and others provided her expert medical attention, all without fee. Sister Dietrich, who had stayed in the home of her sister while here, was most appreciative of the many kindnesses extended to her. She is a lovely lady. She indicated she was anxious to return to her dear husband and family. I thought to myself, *Isn't it a tragedy that political differences cause members of families to have such a difficult time to meet together in today's world.*

Sister Dietrich later reported that when she returned home, she said to her husband, "Dr. Nelson has given me a new heart," whereupon her husband said, "Dr. Nelson has given me a new wife!"

SATURDAY, FEBRUARY 27, 1982

Early this morning I flew to Berlin, where I was met by Regional Representative Hans Ringger arriving from Basel, Switzerland. We rented a car and then drove across Checkpoint Charlie into the German Democratic Republic and then to the little town of Freiberg, where we inspected a proposed building site, even though dusk had blurred our vision of the site.

We then drove to the city of Karl-Marx-Stadt, formerly known as Chemnitz, and stayed at the Chemnitzer Hof Hotel. I thought it interesting that while the Communists have changed the name of the city from Chemnitz to Karl-Marx-Stadt, the hotel continues to bear the Chemnitz name. A stamp was missing from our visas, so our passports were taken, that they might receive proper scrutiny by the police officials and have the proper stamp placed on the visas. It is always frightening to give up one's visa in a Communist-controlled country.

Later in the evening we held a meeting at the home of

Henry and Inge Burkhardt. What delightful people! Their homes in Germany are cold and dreary, as well as drab and in need of repair as pertains to the outside and the entry area. However, when you open the door to the apartment where people live, then the apartment is nicely furnished and is most commodious. This is due to the fact that under the Communist government, landlords are not allowed to increase rent; hence, the common area of a building deteriorates, and individuals are permitted to add what niceties they are able to in the immediate area where they live.

Our meeting began with some refreshments, after which we held discussions which lasted until near midnight. Inasmuch as I do not speak German, it takes twice as long for meetings to be held, the necessary translation of questions and answers occupying a good share of the time.

Frances had sent a lovely new skirt to Sister Burkhardt, as well as a beautiful little china plate bearing the image of a mother and son, a replica of a Relief Society monument. I brought with me a pocket calculator, which I gave to Henry Burkhardt's son Tobias. He was elated, there being nothing in East Germany similar to a pocket calculator. He is about fifteen years of age. I also carried a large cashmere overcoat made in England, which I had purchased in Canada during the years I served there as a mission president. It had been scarcely worn, being too heavy for use generally in Salt Lake City. They assured me there would be someone among our membership in the Dresden Mission who would be overjoyed to receive this beautiful coat.

SUNDAY, FEBRUARY 28, 1982

This morning we drove to Freiberg once again and saw the site selected for a temple there. All of the buildings in

72

Freiberg are ancient and dilapidated. This is a university city where Henry D. Moyle studied following his mission in Germany. New apartment buildings, though stereotyped and somewhat drab in appearance, are planned to be constructed across the street from our site. The site is situated in a corridor rather adjacent to the cities of Dresden, Leipzig, and Karl-Marx-Stadt, which comprise the bulk of our leadership in this land. The city is enjoying an anniversary event next year; hence, the government is willing to make the temple site available on a very long-term lease, that we might construct a building. This is about the only breakthrough we have had with the government in the obtaining of a site on which a new building could be built. I do hope that our project will not be strangled in red tape, for our members desperately need the services which the building would provide.

We then drove to the city of Annaberg, Germany, where we held a district conference. The location of our building once again is in an older setting somewhat back from the street. After you enter the building, however, you notice that it is beautifully appointed. What a delight to be with the members. One good German brother came forward and said that he had a dream the night before that I would be in attendance. He embraced me and bore his testimony. All of the members looked with astonishment as Brother Ringger and I accompanied the mission presidency to the podium. They had not been told that we were coming, which, of necessity, is the procedure for such a visit in this Communist country.

This was the district conference of the Karl-Marx-Stadt District. As the meeting began, I noticed that a man about fifty or fifty-five years of age left his coveted seat on the front row, went to the rear of the building, and helped an elderly man walk up the aisle, giving to him the front-row seat. The good samaritan then went to the rear of the filled building and found a seat. My talk's title and subject was "Love of Neighbor." I used, among others, the illustration of the kindness of this good brother in helping the elderly person to the front. I could not help but notice him in the rear of the building as he took from his pocket his handkerchief and wiped the tears from his eyes. I felt inspired.

I never return from the Dresden Mission without being uplifted. Our activity there is in the 80 percent range, even though we are severely curtailed with respect to the literature and handbooks, etc., we can distribute. Our biggest problem is that our numbers are declining, since missionary work is nonexistent, other than a little part-time effort which our members are able to devote when others demonstrate an interest and ask for further information regarding the Church. We are now down to about 3,700 members from the approximately 4,700 which we had in 1968 when I first received the assignment to this part of the world.

I consider my service in the Dresden Mission to be a highlight in my ministry thus far as a member of the Council of the Twelve. I have seen the people grow and mature and take their places in the Church. The full program as far as the government permits is now in effect in the Dresden Mission. The privilege of the leaders of the mission to come to Salt Lake City and to participate in leadership sessions, attend the temple, and otherwise receive the motivation that comes from the gathering of the Saints here at conference time has, I think, been one of the salutary benefits of the attention provided. Were it not for the continuity established by having one member of the Council of the Twelve monitor and watch over this particular area, I do not believe we would have made nearly the progress we have. Perhaps an additional reason for such progress is my keen love for the German people and the country itself. Above all, the credit belongs to the Lord and to the faith and devotion of our members.

After the conference sessions, I felt impressed to set apart two new counselors to the district president, President Werner Adler. He was so pleased with the fact that we had come to his district that he must have embraced me six times during the course of the conference. These two counselors are fine-looking men. Their wives and families had gathered together in the little Relief Society room, which, incidentally, was not heated due to a desire to conserve fuel. I instructed them and then officiated in setting them apart. Once again I felt prompted that this was something I should do. I then had the privilege of ordaining a young man to the office of elder.

I had some chewing gum in my pocket, so I gave a stick to each of the children of the leadership. They were elated, not having had the opportunity to enjoy such an American delicacy heretofore. Two young teenage girls, daughters of our executive secretary, were in attendance. They were very pretty and shy, as are most girls in similar circumstances wherever we meet them. I dug deeper in my pockets and found a package of Doublemint gum and one of Spearmint gum, which I gave to these two young ladies. You would think I had given them a gift of great value.

We then drove the long distance from Annaberg to Berlin and to the airport, where I caught my plane for London, and Brother Ringger caught his plane for Basel. The connecting plane in Bremen, Germany, was delayed; hence, I arrived in London about two hours beyond the normal time of arrival. I went into the city and registered at the Lowndes Hotel.

MONDAY, APRIL 5, 1982

This morning Robert Hales, Burke Peterson, Hans Ringger, and I met with the First Presidency relative to the temple building project in the Dresden Mission.

FRIDAY, AUGUST 27, 1982

This morning, following assignments in Germany, Frances and I flew to Zurich, where we had an hour together in the departure lounge. Then I took the plane to Berlin and Frances flew to Salt Lake City by way of New York.

When I arrived in Berlin, I was met by Hans Ringger and Robert Hales. We crossed the border and stayed at a hotel in East Berlin. Hans Ringger has developed a system to cross the border, using the facilities of the hotel, which provides them Western money and provides us easier access.

SATURDAY, AUGUST 28, 1982

This morning we drove to Leipzig and inspected two parcels of property which the government has made available for purchase. They are both good sites. We then drove on to Dresden, arriving about noon. A youth conference had just concluded. The young people hesitated leaving. They are so well-mannered and devoted to the gospel. I had the opportunity to greet each one and then felt impressed to stand on the steps and deliver a brief message of encouragement to them. At the conclusion, I mentioned that when I was there previously, I had given several of the young people some American chewing gum, which they seemed to enjoy; hence, I had brought fifteen packages with me, that each might have a sample. One would have thought it was Christmas Day.

We then spent the entire afternoon interviewing priesthood leaders and putting in place the officers for the Freiberg German Democratic Republic Stake.

The local brethren were so humble and devoted to the Lord that they inspired us.

We appointed as president of the new stake Frank Herbert Apel, an automobile electrical systems supervisor. He is about forty-two years of age and has served eighteen years as a counselor in the district presidency and most recently as the executive secretary of the Dresden Mission. He has a lovely wife and four children. His first counselor is Heinz Koschnicke, who is a supervisor of trades; and his second counselor is Reimund Dörlitz.

Several interesting experiences occurred as these brethren were appointed. Brother Dörlitz had a mustache, which I felt should be trimmed if he were to retain it. I told Brother Henry Burkhardt that it would be best if we didn't make a major issue of it. He said he would take care of it. I even suggested that he wait a week or two before bringing it up. Fifteen minutes later he returned and said, "Brother Dörlitz will have no mustache tomorrow. He wants to be like others of the brethren." Brother Dörlitz is forty-three years of age, having served twenty-one years as a branch president.

When I met with the brethren and their wives to tell them that there would be a conference in Salt Lake City to which they would be invited, together with their companions, Sister Koschnicke could not refrain from weeping tears of joy, with the thought that she and her husband could receive their endowments and be sealed.

Rudi Lehmann was called as stake patriarch. He has served for sixteen years as president of his district. When I complimented him for his untiring service, he responded in broken English, "I did all these things for the Lord." He then said that after the war he met an American serviceman who was a member of the Church. "Had he spoken to me about the Church," said Brother Lehmann, "I could have been a member much sooner."

SUNDAY, AUGUST 29, 1982

Today I created the Freiberg German Democratic Republic Stake of The Church of Jesus Christ of Latter-day Saints. Approximately eighteen hundred members in the Karl-Marx-Stadt and Dresden Districts came together to form the stake. We had just under one thousand members in attendance for this historic occasion. A Brother Wilfred Möller, an excellent interpreter, a professor of English from Dortmund, joined us and served as my interpreter.

This was a day never to be forgotten, for today prophecy was fulfilled. At my second visit to the Dresden Mission, I stood at the pulpit and told the people I had never seen greater faith and that surely the Lord would reward such faith by providing every blessing that other members of the Church would receive. I have seen the step-by-step unfolding of this prophecy and know it came from the Lord.

At the conclusion of our meetings, I had a visit with our senior high councilor, Brother Werner Adler. He is a large man, both in heart and in size. He has served nineteen years as a district president. He and his wife were invited by the Church, over a year ago, to attend conference, but since the Adlers have no children, the government no doubt was fearful they would not return, and therefore they would not grant a visa to Sister Adler. Brother Adler felt he did not want to come without his dear wife.

In a plaintive fashion, they asked whether he would ever again have an opportunity to receive an invitation to

Renate and Werner Adler of Plauen,
German Democratic Republic

conference, now that the stake was formed and he no longer served as a district president. I turned to him and said that if it was within my power to grant it, he would receive such an invitation and that I would do all that I could to ensure that such was forthcoming. The important thing will be whether or not his government will alter its position and permit visas to be granted.

I noticed that Brother Adler's clothing, though well kept, was rather old. I struck upon the idea that perhaps my suit would fit him. I tried upon him the suit jacket. He was so pleased and said that it fit just fine. I then put on a pair

*August 1982: Frank Apel (left) is president of the newly created
Freiberg Germany Stake, and Rudi Lehmann is stake patriarch.*

of slacks and a jacket and left my suit with Brother Adler. I
also left several ties and a shirt. He was overjoyed. I then
turned to Brother Lehmann, the patriarch, and placed my
shoe along one of his and said, "Would these shoes fit you?"
He looked and then said sadly, "No, they're a little large."
Then his eyes brightened, and he said in English, "They will
fit my son!" I then gave him the shoes for his son.

I had a small pocket calculator in my briefcase which I
showed to our new stake president and asked him if he had
a calculator. He, of course, answered in the negative. I then
asked if he would like this one. He, too, was pleased.

After setting apart the officers and holding a brief orientation meeting for them, we returned to Berlin and
crossed the border to the West.

I never visit the Saints in East Germany without returning a better person. Elders Harold B. Lee and Spencer W.
Kimball, as members of the Council of the Twelve, each
made the comment at the time the Dresden Mission was
created, "I hope the day will come when we can have a
stake in that part of the world." That day is today.

WEDNESDAY, SEPTEMBER 1, 1982

In my office following the meeting of the Twelve, we
held a meeting relative to the new temple at Freiberg,
Germany. How I long for this building, which will then provide our Saints the opportunity to be endowed and sealed.
The way has been miraculously opened up for a parcel of
property to be obtained, and permission is moving forward
relative to the plans for construction.

TUESDAY, SEPTEMBER 14, 1982

Met early this morning with the First Presidency relative to our proposed temple in the German Democratic
Republic. The Brethren gave their go-ahead for the building, with an additional amount of space to be provided, for
which I am grateful.

TUESDAY, OCTOBER 5, 1982

In the late afternoon I held the semiannual meeting of
those concerned with the Dresden Mission. It was delightful
to meet with Henry Burkhardt and others to review the sta-
tus of our proposed temple and stake center and to otherwise pursue the work of the Lord in this part of the world.

WEDNESDAY, OCTOBER 6, 1982

Attended a meeting of the Priesthood Executive Council,

after which I met with Bishop Sellner, a fine young bishop from the Freiberg German Democratic Republic Stake and former director of our seminaries there. He and his two sisters visited with me in my office. One of the sisters is a resident of Salt Lake City and had been able to obtain permission for her brother and sister to visit her on her birthday.

SATURDAY, OCTOBER 9, 1982

I attended the Saturday sessions of the Riverton Utah Stake conference.

In the evening I spoke to the subject of tithing and home teaching, using Walter Krause and Johann Denndorfer as an example. Brother Denndorfer had been converted to the Church in Germany, and following World War II, he found himself virtually a prisoner in his own land—the land of Hungary. How he wanted to visit the temple! How he desired to receive his spiritual blessings. Request after request was denied, and he almost despaired. Then his home teacher visited. Brother Walter Krause went from the northeastern portion of Germany all the way to Hungary. He had said to his home teaching companion, "Would you like to go home teaching with me this week?"

His companion said, "When will we leave?"

"Tomorrow," replied Brother Krause.

"When will we come back?" asked the companion.

"Oh, in about a week—if we get back!"

And away they went to visit Brother Denndorfer. He had not had home teachers since before the war. Now, when he saw the servants of the Lord, he was overwhelmed. He did not shake hands with them; rather, he went to his bedroom and took from a secret hiding place his tithing that he had saved from the day he became a member of the Church and returned to Hungary. He gave this tithing to his home teachers and said, "Now I am current with the Lord. Now I feel worthy to shake the hand of servants of the Lord!"

Brother Krause asked him about his desire to attend the temple in Switzerland. He said, "It is no use. I have tried and tried. The government has even confiscated my Church books—my greatest treasure."

Brother Krause, an ordained patriarch, provided Brother Denndorfer with a patriarchal blessing. At the conclusion of the blessing, he said to Brother Denndorfer, "Try again." And Brother Denndorfer submitted the request once again to the authorities. This time approval came, and with joy Brother Denndorfer went to the Swiss Temple and stayed almost a month. He received his own endowment, his deceased wife was sealed to him, and he was able to do the work for 785 of his ancestors. He returned to his home renewed in body and spirit.

The membership of the Riverton Stake enjoyed this very faith-promoting example.

SUNDAY, OCTOBER 10, 1982

Last evening I felt impressed to invite Walter and Edith Krause, who are visiting in Salt Lake City, to attend with me the morning session of the Riverton Utah Stake conference. This I did. The Krauses thrilled the population of the stake with their moving testimonies. Gary Schwendiman served as interpreter.

In the second session of the conference, I invited President and Sister Henry Burkhardt to attend, with John Fetzer being their interpreter. Once again the people were overjoyed. It was the largest attendance the Riverton stake had ever experienced. The theme naturally turned to the special announcement which appeared in Saturday evening's *Church News* to the effect that a temple of the Lord would be built in Freiberg, German Democratic Republic. There is a moving drama behind this announcement. Perhaps my journal should record some of the details.

From the time of my first visit to the German Democratic Republic, I felt that the people, through their worthiness, should receive all the blessings which membership in the Church provides. In fact, in a district conference I prophesied, under the influence of the Spirit, that through their faithfulness, they would receive every blessing. This was later confirmed in an experience wherein I attended a special conference session in Dresden, German Democratic Republic, and on the Saturday evening felt impressed that early the next morning I should dedicate the land for the preaching of the gospel and the establishment of the work of the Lord. I realized that this land had never been formally dedicated since World War II, when it came into existence under its new name and government. I had just concluded dedicating the land of Portugal and had experienced a remarkable outpouring of the Spirit of the Lord on that occasion.

On the morning following the Saturday evening session, several of us gathered on a high mountaintop, and I offered a dedicatory prayer, which was confirmed in its entirety by the Spirit of the Lord.

As Henry Burkhardt spoke in the Riverton stake conference, he reiterated what he had said earlier to a special meeting of the First Presidency—namely, that many elements of that dedicatory prayer had been fulfilled and that this had indeed been the dawning of a new day for the Church in the German Democratic Republic. Brother

Burkhardt then went on to say that the announcement of the temple continued a series of miracles: for example, private ownership of property is not permitted in that country, and yet we have been granted private ownership. The building of a temple has never before been permitted in a Communist nation. In this case, the government itself suggested the building of the temple as an alternative to considering our request that members be permitted to visit the temple in Zollikofen, Switzerland. A third miracle is that our land was purchased with German Democratic Republic marks rather than with currency from the Western nations. All in all, the event has been miraculous.

The architects from the Church have been working with the architects of the German Democratic Republic, and now it appears that we are ready to proceed with the temple. On a lovely four-acre site which I have inspected, we shall build a temple of the Lord, as well as a beautiful stake center.

This is the information which Henry and Inge Burkhardt included in their remarks to the people of the Riverton stake. It was one of the most spiritual stake conferences I have ever attended.

SATURDAY, DECEMBER 11, 1982

Laird Snelgrove hosted the ambassador from the German Democratic Republic, taking him to Snowbird and other points of interest. It is service like this that often goes unthanked and unacknowledged, and I am grateful that we have men like Brother Snelgrove and others to assist us.

6

"Open Up the Way to Thy Holy Temple"

THE FREIBERG TEMPLE AND
A SECOND STAKE
1983–85

WEDNESDAY, MARCH 30, 1983

In the late afternoon I had the privilege of performing the sealing ceremony for President and Sister Frank Apel of the Freiberg German Democratic Republic Stake. This was a sheer delight. Tears of gratitude flowed freely. Thelma Fetzer attended, as did Gary Schwendiman and others who have served with the choice people of the Dresden Mission.

WEDNESDAY, APRIL 6, 1983

In the evening Frances and I hosted a dinner for President and Sister Frank Apel and President and Sister Henry Burkhardt, our official visitors from the German Democratic Republic—from the Freiberg Stake and the Dresden Mission, respectively. We invited to be in attendance Brother and Sister Enzio Busche, President and Sister Robert Hales, Brother and Sister John Fetzer, Brother and Sister Gary Schwendiman, and Thelma Fetzer. We had a delightful time. We missed, however, the physical presence of our beloved associate, Percy K. Fetzer. He would have been there had he been permitted to tarry in mortality.

FRIDAY, APRIL 22, 1983

Journeyed to Berlin, where I was met by Hans Ringger, our Regional Representative.

We were then taken across Checkpoint Charlie and stayed at the Hotel Metropol in East Berlin.

SATURDAY, APRIL 23, 1983

Drove today to Wittenberg and saw the church where Martin Luther nailed to the door his famous proclamation. A substantial crowd of people viewed the tourist attraction on this lovely and sun-drenched day. An English-speaking guide was most gracious. She would not accept any contribution for herself, simply suggesting that any contribution could go toward the maintenance of the church. We made a contribution for this purpose.

At 2:00 P.M. I had the privilege to preside at the ground breaking for the Freiberg Germany Temple. This is a miracle of miracles! I think it all began when we made a final effort with the government to get permission for our faithful couples to go to the Swiss Temple. The minister in their government then said, "Why not build a temple in our country?" We took him up on his offer, and the building is now under way.

Elder Robert D. Hales, Hans B. Ringger, Emil Fetzer, Amos Wright, and I had journeyed to Freiberg for this occasion. The weather was beautiful. I had previously given Bishop Hales the assignment, with tongue in cheek, to take care of the weather. I said to him, "Elder Hales, the Lord has opened the way for a temple to be erected here in this land

We joyfully participate in official ground-breaking ceremonies for the Freiberg Germany Temple. Foreground, left to right: Elder Hans B. Ringger, Dr. Dieter Hantzsche of the Building Academy of Dresden, Emil B. Fetzer, Elder Robert D. Hales, Elder Thomas S. Monson, Elder F. Enzio Busche, and Dr. Vetter, vice chairman of the County Council of Freiberg.

far away from freedom, and you have the opportunity now, per my assignment, to be in charge of the weather. I would like you to ensure that we have sunshine to shine upon all who are in attendance for this great occasion!"

A lovely stand had been erected for the official party, and though we had not made any public announcement, since there was a feeling this was in the best interests of the work, there nonetheless was a nice crowd assembled. As I took shovel in hand and prepared to turn the soil, a member of the Church Building Department said, "Be careful how you lean on the shovel. When Brother Packer broke ground for a new temple in another country, the shovel broke under the weight of his foot." I responded, "German-made shovels don't break."

I am overwhelmed with a deep sense of gratitude as I offer a prayer of dedication upon the site where the Freiberg Temple will be constructed.

We went forward with the proceedings, after which it was my opportunity to offer a prayer of dedication on the ground, setting it apart for its special purpose to accommodate a house of the Lord.

We purposely restricted the amount of people in attendance, having just thirty or forty Church officers and their families. We also had visitors from East Germany's Department of Religion and the Architectural Institute, the building contractors in Berlin, and other dignitaries. I think it significant that when I invited all of them to close their eyes and bow their heads that I might dedicate the building, they did so. Brother Von Selchow, our seminary and institute leader, opened his eyes during the prayer and noted that every person there except one had his head bowed. I think this is most significant, considering that the government of the nation is Communist.

We then met at the Freiberg chapel with representatives of the government's architectural division, where we made plans for a temple president's residence on property nearby the temple and stake center site. We also looked at preliminary plans for a building proposed for the Leipzig Branch.

We then returned to Berlin, crossed Checkpoint Charlie, and then went to the downtown section, where I registered at the Schweizerhof Hotel.

I left the German Democratic Republic rejoicing in my heart and soul, now that a temple of God has been approved for construction and the dedication of the ground accomplished.

TUESDAY, JANUARY 10, 1984

Early this morning I met with Robert Hales and Dean Larsen relative to matters in the German Democratic Republic. It now appears that we will attempt to move toward placing the balance of the membership in that country in a second stake, thereby, through the two stakes, accommodating our approximately thirty-seven hundred members. In addition, Brother Hales thinks we could make some effort toward having local full-time missionaries. A problem is that our population is aging, and deaths of members exceed births. When outward emigration of individuals who are over sixty-five occurs, this also compounds the problem of our membership base.

MONDAY, APRIL 9, 1984

This morning I held the traditional conference meeting

of those involved with the German Democratic Republic. We had a fine session.

The temple is progressing in Freiberg, German Democratic Republic, and permission has been granted for a stake center to be erected in the city of Leipzig. I am elated with the progress.

SATURDAY, JUNE 2, 1984

Flew to Berlin, where I met Hans Ringger and Robert Hales and spent a delightful day visiting the temple, which is under construction at Freiberg, German Democratic Republic. The exterior of the two buildings is about complete. The interior, of course, remains to be completed. It is anticipated that the buildings will be ready for dedication in April of 1985. The government architect met with me and explained that if we would build patron housing units on a two-acre plot immediately adjacent to the temple, he would make arrangements for the government to sell the property to us at a most favorable price. Property is simply not made available every day in this country, and the restriction of building a suitable structure is mandated before the property transfer is made. We also saw the temple president's home, which is under construction, after which we viewed a beautiful piece of property in Dresden on which a chapel will be built, and then visited the site in Leipzig where a stake center is about to be constructed.

Throughout the afternoon and evening we conducted interviews relating to the creation of the Leipzig stake.

When we entered the Leipzig chapel, I was amazed that all of the priesthood brethren who had assembled for our interviews were singing. These brethren love to sing. It is almost as though there has been a time warp take place in their lives. They are unpolluted by the softness and degeneracy which one sees in many countries, including our own. There is no pornography or drug use, and while freedoms are restricted, our Church members seem to draw closer together in unity and combined faith. They are as pure a group of priesthood brethren as I have ever met. The only equal happens to be the priesthood brethren whom I interviewed prior to the creation of the Freiberg stake.

We made our selection of a stake presidency. Brother Manfred Schutze is the president, Brother Gerhard Müller is the first counselor, and Brother Gurgen Pabst is the second counselor.

In the late evening we returned to the hotel. We had excellent interpreters with us, Brother Fischer and Brother Möller, who came from Frankfurt and Dortmund respectively. Brother Möller has been my interpreter on previous occasions. He speaks with a British accent, and they tell me he is an excellent interpreter.

SUNDAY, JUNE 3, 1984

Attended the organization meetings of the Leipzig German Democratic Republic Stake. With the creation of the Leipzig stake, all of the members of the Church in the German Democratic Republic now reside in either the Freiberg or Leipzig stake. I dissolved the Germany Dresden Mission, which I had created on June 14, 1969, giving it a fifteen-year history almost to the day. I shall ever remember that occasion, when Percy K. Fetzer and I officiated at the organizational meetings, naming Henry Burkhardt, Walter Krause, and Gottfried Richter as the mission presidency. The only person whom we ordained a high priest on that occasion was Brother Burkhardt, feeling that it was a worthwhile thing, in such an organization, to have only the president hold the office of high priest. I remember that when I returned to Salt Lake City following the creation of the Dresden Mission, both Harold B. Lee and Spencer W. Kimball voiced their hope that the mission organization would be a forerunner to stakes of Zion, which provide more stability and growth opportunities for the membership of the Church. Today witnessed the fulfillment of their dream. While Percy Fetzer has been called home to his Heavenly Father, I felt his presence and noted the significant contribution he had made to the work of the Lord in this country.

As Henry Burkhardt was speaking to the congregation and expressing his appreciation for the privilege of serving the people of that area, the members of the congregation were visibly moved to tears.

When it was my opportunity to speak, I mentioned that the Dresden Mission had been created on June 14, 1969, and dissolved on June 3, 1984. It has served as a forerunner of the stake organization, exactly as had been hoped by the brethren of the First Presidency and Council of the Twelve. As I spoke I felt prompted to present to Henry Burkhardt publicly, in behalf of the entire congregation as well as the General Authorities, my personal leather-bound set of scriptures. I indicated that these same scriptures were with me when the Dresden Mission was organized and at the various mission and district conferences held over the years. They were with me at the creation of the Freiberg stake, the inspirational ceremonies pertaining to the dedication of the land with a special blessing upon the members of the Church, and the ground breaking for the Freiberg Temple, and now the creation of the Leipzig Stake—each event a miraculous occurrence. I indicated that Brother Burkhardt could follow in my English edition of my scriptures his German edition and thereby improve his English and know the passages which I particularly treasure and have underlined in my personal set. It was a moving experience, and while it will deprive me of a well-used and carefully prepared set of standard works, I can't think of a better place to have these scriptures than with Henry Burkhardt and his family. I did so willingly and have no regrets.

As part of my talk I cited scriptures pertaining to Zion, such as Doctrine and Covenants 68:25–26, 82:14, and 109:39 and 59. I pointed out that they were entitled to all of the blessings which the Lord promised to those who had assembled at Zion and that our Heavenly Father has manifest His love for them in making available to them all of the blessings of Church membership.

It was with a heart filled with gratitude that I left Leipzig today, crossed the border into West Berlin, and flew to London, England.

MONDAY, JUNE 4, 1984

Returned from London to New York and thence to Salt Lake City.

THURSDAY, JULY 5, 1984

Today Neal Maxwell, Burke Peterson, Joseph Wirthlin, and I held meetings with all of the employees in the Frankfurt offices of the Church.

After the meetings were over, we had dinner at a nearby restaurant. On the way back to the hotel, I recognized Dr. Dieter Hantzsche from the architectural academy of the German Democratic Republic. We crossed over the street to greet him. Dr. Hantzsche inferred that things were not going well at the moment, which prompted me to invite him to speak to me privately and candidly relative to the work of our church in the German Democratic Republic. We learned that there had been too many Church visitors to that country and that the government was confused with respect to the stake organizations and the new role of Henry Burkhardt. Further, with the construction of the temple, the stake center at Freiberg, the projected stake center at Leipzig, and a building at Dresden, they knew that the influence of the Church was more visible than it had heretofore been. We were able to make plans for the necessary orientation meetings and the drawing up of a set of governing procedures, such as the Articles of Faith, which will give the government a general view of the objectives and purposes of the Church.

I think it was more than a coincidence that we should meet Dr. Hantzsche during his visit to Frankfurt.

THURSDAY, JULY 26, 1984

Early this morning I met with Emil Fetzer, Joseph Wirthlin, and Burke Peterson to plan for the temple housing in Freiberg, where those who are assigned to work in the temple will require modest apartments. We felt good about our recommendation. Let us hope that it will be approved.

TUESDAY, AUGUST 28, 1984

A full day of meetings in Frankfurt, Germany, with respect to our area presidency work there and, most particularly, refining a "statement of purpose" message which the government of the German Democratic Republic has requested from us. It appears that with our new buildings dominating the landscape of certain cities in the German Democratic Republic, congregations of other churches have become envious and have protested to the government as to why they cannot have priority and materials to repair their leaking roofs and otherwise decorate their buildings. This has occasioned the government to ask us for an official statement of purpose so that they, in turn, can assure members of other congregations that we have not grown in number and that we, ourselves, are providing the financial resources to upgrade our buildings.

Late in the afternoon I took the plane from Frankfurt en route to New York and thence to Salt Lake City. Because of the time zone changes, it is possible to travel a great many miles and still not tick off a proportionate number of hours on the clock.

MONDAY, SEPTEMBER 17, 1984

Flew from London, England, to New York and then from New York to Chicago and Chicago to Salt Lake City, arriving in the late afternoon.

Upon arrival in Salt Lake, I felt impressed to visit with President Hinckley relative to the "statement of purpose" document which had been prepared by our legal counsel in Frankfurt, Germany, in consultation with our legal counsel from the German Democratic Republic. I read the document to Brother Hinckley, and he made just one word change before approving the document to be sent to the governmental authorities of the German Democratic Republic. This was a most unusual situation and I am grateful that I followed the promptings of the Spirit, even though I was somewhat weary from a long plane journey all the way from Europe.

97

In October 1984, construction of the Freiberg Germany Temple
is steadily progressing.

MONDAY, OCTOBER 8, 1984

This morning I took care of a host of details at the office. Henry and Inge Burkhardt are here from the German Democratic Republic to receive orientation relative to their new assignments as temple president and temple matron for the Freiberg Germany Temple. I had a lovely visit with them this afternoon, along with Brother Norbert Lehnig. Brother Lehnig is a dental technician and comes from the German Democratic Republic. He is so good to all of our visitors from Germany in sharing his home, his talents, and his time.

TUESDAY, NOVEMBER 27, 1984

In the afternoon I met with Henry and Inge Burkhardt as they prepared to return to their home in the German Democratic Republic. It has been a delight for these people to be in Salt Lake City for six weeks receiving the training necessary for their new duties as temple president and matron of the Freiberg Temple. They are truly persons without guile and totally dedicated to the work of the Lord.

SUNDAY, DECEMBER 2, 1984

Early this morning I flew to Frankfurt, Germany, where I spent the entire day with Joseph and Elisa Wirthlin discussing matters relating to the Europe area. Brother Wirthlin had many items to review with me.

In the evening we drove to the Airport Sheraton Hotel, where we met Hans Ringger, who had just returned from meetings in Poland and Yugoslavia. We had a lengthy agenda relating to matters at the Freiberg Germany Temple. We are ever grateful for the work of Hans Ringger. I believe the Lord has raised him up with his unique background, his sweet spirit of devotion to the gospel, his outstanding abilities, and his Swiss citizenship which permits him access to the hearts and to some countries which would not welcome so freely citizens from the West.

MONDAY, DECEMBER 3, 1984

Spent the entire day returning from Frankfurt via London and Chicago.

WEDNESDAY, JANUARY 23, 1985

This morning Hans Ringger, Joseph Wirthlin, and I crossed the border into East Berlin, where we met Henry Burkhardt.

We then paid a visit to the state secretary, Minister Gysi. I was impressed with this civil servant. He knew a great deal about our church and spoke fluent English. He asked,

"How is it that your church is sufficiently rich to construct buildings in our country?" I answered that the Church is not rich, but that we follow the ancient biblical principal of tithing. This and the fact that our church has no paid ministry, I advised, were two reasons why we were able to build the buildings now under way, including the beautiful temple at Freiberg. Immediately Minister Gysi turned to his aide and said, "These are two important points. I think our church has ten thousand paid priests. No wonder we are short of money."

After a leisurely period of time with Minister Gysi, he complimented us on our statement of purpose document which had been previously submitted, and he offered whatever help he could to make our temple dedication the success we anticipate it will be. I felt pleased with Minister Gysi's attitude.

I then flew to London, arriving late in the evening.

WEDNESDAY, MARCH 27, 1985

After a full day at the office, I had the delightful experience of going to the Jordan River Temple, there to perform the sealing ceremony for Karl Heinz Friedrich Leonhardt and his wife, Brigitte Ursula Danisch Leonhardt. Brother and Sister Leonhardt are residents of the German Democratic Republic. Brother Leonhardt has been called to serve as the recorder in the Freiberg Temple. These are choice Latter-day Saints. While they speak but little English, through the aid of Gary Schwendiman, my interpreter, we were able to communicate and had a wonderful time together. Also in attendance were Donovan Van Dam, president of the Jordan River Temple, and Frank Apel, president of the Freiberg DDR Stake.

Crowds lined up to tour the Freiberg Temple during the open house. Before the temple's dedication, approximately ninety thousand people attended the open house.

WEDNESDAY, JUNE 5, 1985

Received an outstanding report from Joseph Wirthlin indicating that in the first three days of the open house at Freiberg, Germany, relative to the new temple which has been constructed there, the attendance totaled 18,440.

TUESDAY, JUNE 25, 1985

This morning we flew to London, England, arriving in the early evening.

WEDNESDAY, JUNE 26, 1985

Today we flew to Berlin, Germany, where we were met by Joseph and Elisa Wirthlin and President and Sister Dieter Berndt of the Berlin stake. We held meetings relative to the forthcoming dedicatory ceremonies and otherwise took care of last-minute planning.

101

THURSDAY, JUNE 27, 1985

Today President and Sister Gordon B. Hinckley, together with their party, arrived in Berlin and all of us boarded a specially arranged bus for the border crossing and travel to Dresden in the German Democratic Republic.

After a pleasant drive over the autobahn, we arrived in Dresden and were accommodated in a lovely new hotel which the government had erected in the ancient city of Dresden. The evidence of the British and American fire bombings of World War II is still everywhere to be seen. It is sad to recall that some three hundred thousand people were killed on that terrible night toward the end of World War II. Refugees were traveling through the city in an effort to be ahead of the approaching Russian troops; hence, there was an unusually large number of persons in the city the night of the bombing. The government has simply abandoned the older section of town, which was most heavily bombed, and has rebuilt Dresden to the side of the devastated area.

FRIDAY, JUNE 28, 1985

This morning we departed Dresden en route to Freiberg for a busy day of activities.

At the beautiful Freiberg Germany Temple we hosted a tour for government officials from the ministry in Berlin and from Dresden. The men and their wives seemed much impressed with what we had to offer. We showed them the same film, explaining temple activities, which had been shown to all those who attended the open house.

The open house, in and of itself, was a miraculous event. To the astonishment of everyone, almost ninety thousand persons visited the temple. When one considers that our total Church population in the German Democratic Republic is only approximately forty-seven hundred, it is all the more amazing. Some waited in line up to two and three hours, holding umbrellas or newspapers over their heads to protect themselves from the rain. Several were asked, "Why do you stand in line to visit a temple of the Mormon Church?" The response was simply, "Because I want to. I don't mind standing in line when it is my choice."

In the prayer of dedication which I some years ago offered in behalf of the German Democratic Republic and our Church activities there, I asked our Heavenly Father to instill within the citizenry a curiosity concerning the Church and a desire to learn more of our teachings. I consider the successful open house to be a direct fulfillment and response of our Heavenly Father to that particular prayer.

After the tour, cornerstone laying ceremonies were held. The official party was seated in the temple, with an overflow audience in the Freiberg Ward chapel, located adjacent to the temple. After the official ceremonies, we officiated in the laying of the cornerstone.

During the noon hour, we went to downtown Freiberg, where a luncheon was hosted for our official guests and appropriate thanks expressed. A bronze rendering of a lovely small statue of a pioneer woman posing with her daughter, who is holding a violin, was presented to the mayor of Freiberg. He seemed most grateful. We then returned to Dresden and had dinner there.

SATURDAY, JUNE 29, 1985

Again this morning we journeyed from Dresden to Freiberg, which required about an hour of time. We kept the same bus throughout our entire stay in the German

Left to right: Gottfried Richter, President Gordon B. Hinckley, Elder Hans B. Ringger, Frances J. Monson, Elder Thomas S. Monson, and temple president Henry Burkhardt on the joyous day of the dedication of the Freiberg Temple.

Democratic Republic, and an articulate lady guide was provided by the government. This was ostensibly to provide answers to our questions, but, more particularly, the government surely wished to monitor our activities.

President Gordon B. Hinckley offered a beautiful dedicatory prayer and spoke movingly and with power.

Today marked one of the highlights of my life. To have the opportunity to be the first speaker at the first dedicatory session of the Freiberg Temple was not only a great honor but also the fulfillment of a deep and long-held desire for the wonderful Saints in the German Democratic Republic to have the blessing of a temple. It was difficult for me to control my emotions as I spoke, for racing through my mind were examples of the faith of the devoted Saints of this part

*The Freiberg Germany Temple stands complete and beautiful
at the time of its dedication.*

of the world. Frequently people will ask, "How has it been possible for the Church to obtain permission to build a temple behind the Iron Curtain?" My feeling is simply that the faith and devotion of our Latter-day Saints in that area brought forth the help of Almighty God and provided for them the eternal blessings which they so richly deserve.

The dedication services were filled with rejoicing. The singing was a prayer unto God, the messages were from the heart, and the prayers reflected the feelings and committed testimonies of faithful souls.

In the evening, on the way back to Dresden, I contemplated that it has been seventeen years since I had made my first visit to Germany as a member of the Council of the Twelve. I entered the German Democratic Republic at that time, being the first General Authority so to do since Spencer W. Kimball toured that area in approximately 1958.

Certainly I was the first one to go to our membership there following the erection of the Berlin Wall and the tightening of security on the part of the government. It has been a most enjoyable assignment for me to work with our outstanding members and leaders in this nation. Some of the milestone events were the dedicatory prayer which I offered; the organization of the Dresden Mission and the establishment of districts for training for eventual stakehood; the creation of the Freiberg Stake and, later, the Leipzig Stake; groundbreaking services for the Freiberg Germany Temple and the prayer of dedication which I was privileged to offer on that occasion; and now the culmination: the completion and dedication of a house of the Lord. All honor and glory belong to our Heavenly Father, for it is only through His divine intervention that these events have taken place. I am simply gratified beyond words to have been a part of what I consider one of the most historic and faith-filled chapters of Church history.

SUNDAY, JUNE 30, 1985

Again we continued with temple dedication services. All persons were accommodated within the temple proper by having multiple services, thereby avoiding the necessity of overflow congregations in the adjacent ward chapel.

During the session, I noticed Brother Schult from Berlin sitting on the front row. He is very short in stature but has a tremendous heart. I related how one day I sat with him in the office of President Spencer W. Kimball. This wonderful prophet asked him about the people in his ward. He did not ask about any percentage of activity. He simply said, "Brother Schult, do your members have enough to eat?" And Brother Schult answered affirmatively. Then they stood

Ruth and Hans Schult, short in stature but great in spirit, stand near two tall full-time missionaries, Elders Miles (left) and Tree.

next to one another. They are about the same height. Brother Schult said, "May I embrace you?" And President Kimball responded, "I would love to embrace someone my own size!" Then these two wonderful men embraced one another.

During that same meeting with President Kimball and Brother Schult, another inspirational moment took place. A sister from East Germany was also in the office with President Kimball, Brother Schult, and me. She told how she had looked forward to coming to Dresden on the day that President Kimball was to be there. She had counted the weeks and then the days and then the hours until she would see the prophet of the Lord and hear him—a lifelong, treasured experience. But then her mother took ill, and she could not leave her mother to come to Dresden. She said, "All of my hopes are gone. I shall never see the prophet of the Lord." But she remembered that great commandment, "Honor thy father and thy mother," and she remained at home with her mother. Then, with tears brimming up in her eyes, she said, "Little did I dream, President Kimball, that I would be sitting right here in your office today. Here I can see you more closely than I could have if I had seen you in Dresden."

As she told President Kimball that experience, he stood up, walked around the desk, took her by the hand, and kissed her on the forehead. Then the tears did flow! She had honored her mother, and the Lord had granted a far greater blessing than that which she had ever hoped to receive.

The Relief Society performed beautifully its assignment of providing refreshments between sessions. The table was spread as an artist would paint a scene on canvas. All of the food was artistically displayed, using geometric patterns, even for the placement of the glasses from which we would drink. I have never during my lifetime seen such meticulous care devoted to what some may consider a mundane assignment. To these choice members, however, it was an opportunity to show their gratitude for the General Authorities who had come to them.

In the sessions, several of the speakers from the German Democratic Republic spoke of the prayer which I had the privilege to offer that rainy day on a mountainside, and they expressed their gratitude to our Heavenly Father for the fulfillment of yet another portion of that prayer. It was a day of rich satisfaction for me.

In the early evening we returned to Berlin, staying at the Schweizerhof Hotel in West Berlin. Interestingly, David Kennedy and Lenore Kennedy, who went across the border with Hans Ringger and his wife, returned with us on the bus. When Brother and Sister Ringger left the German Democratic Republic through a different checkpoint, the government officials wanted to know where David Kennedy was. It was only after a two-hour delay that they were able to verify that he had left the country on our bus. This simply illustrates how a person of prominence is carefully monitored during his stay behind the Iron Curtain.

On the bus ride back to West Berlin, with Dieter Berndt accompanying us, I told President Hinckley and the others present of Dieter's service in the Church. I related to them the faith-promoting experience of having Edwin Q. Cannon, Jr., come to my office, indicating he had been pruning his missionary slides. Among those slides he had kept since his mission forty years earlier were several which he could not specifically identify. Every time he had planned to discard them, he had been impressed to keep them, although he was at a loss as to why. They were photographs taken by Brother Cannon when he served in Stettin, Germany, and were of a family—a mother, a father, a small girl, a small boy. He knew their surname was Berndt but could remember nothing more about them. He indicated that he understood there was a Berndt who was a Regional Representative in Germany, and he thought—although he knew the possibility was remote—that this Berndt might have some connection with the Berndts who had lived in Stettin and who were depicted in the photographs. Before disposing of the slides, he thought he would check with me.

I told Brother Cannon I was leaving shortly for Berlin, where I anticipated that I would see Dieter Berndt, the Regional Representative, and that I would show the slides to him to see if there was any relationship and to ask if he wanted them. There was a possibility I would also see

Brother Berndt's sister, who was married to Dietmar Matern, a stake president in Hamburg.

The Lord didn't even let me get to Berlin before His purposes were accomplished. I was in Zurich, Switzerland, boarding the flight to Berlin, when who should also board the plane but Dieter Berndt. He sat next to me, and I told him I had some old slides of people named Berndt from Stettin. I handed them to him and asked if he could identify those shown in the photographs. As he looked at them carefully, he began to weep. He said, "Our family lived in Stettin during the war. My father was killed when an Allied bomb struck the plant where he worked. Not long afterward, the Russians invaded Poland and the area of Stettin. My mother took my sister and me and fled from the advancing enemy. Everything had to be left behind, including any photographs we had. Brother Monson, I am the little boy pictured in these slides, and my sister is the little girl. The man and woman are our dear parents. Until today, I have had no photographs of our childhood in Stettin or of my father."

Wiping away my own tears, I told Brother Berndt the slides were his. He placed them carefully and lovingly in his briefcase. At the next general conference, when Dieter Berndt visited Salt Lake City, he paid a visit to Brother Edwin Cannon, Jr., that he might express in person his gratitude for the inspiration that came to Brother Cannon to retain these precious slides and for the fact that Brother Cannon followed that inspiration in keeping them for forty years.

Brother Berndt mentioned how his wife's father awakened in the middle of the night some years ago and felt impressed to take his family across the border. This he did, just before the erection of the Berlin Wall. He later became the patriarch of the Berlin Stake. When I named him as

patriarch, I did not know that he was the father-in-law of
our then stake president, Dieter Berndt, nor did I know the
miraculous manner in which the Lord had preserved him
and his family during the terrible period of World War II
and, likewise, the inspiration which permitted him to locate
in West Berlin.

MONDAY, JULY 1, 1985

Today our official party boarded the airplane and flew
to Frankfurt, Germany, where we were met and taken to
Friedrichsdorf, which is a suburb of Frankfurt. Here we participated in ground-breaking ceremonies for the new temple
to be erected. The press from Salt Lake City from the three
television stations had been present in the German
Democratic Republic and also for this event. A spokesman
for the town was most complimentary, indicating that
Friedrichsdorf had opened its arms to fleeing religious
Huguenots years before who had come to the area, and they
were happy, in that same tradition of religious freedom, to
welcome The Church of Jesus Christ of Latter-day Saints. It
was a day to be remembered.

In the evening we flew to Stockholm, where we were
met by Bo Wennerlund and Sister Wennerlund and taken to
accommodations in the area where the temple has been
constructed.

SATURDAY, AUGUST 10, 1985

Flew from New York to London, and after a two-hour
layover took a British Airways flight to Hamburg.

SUNDAY, AUGUST 11, 1985

I took a taxi from the hotel to the airport early this

morning. Hamburg was beautiful this morning, with bright sunshine reflecting on the inlet waterways and the meticulously kept parks of this large industrial city. Hamburg suffered devastating air raids during World War II, in which many of its citizens perished. The Guertler family, who settled in the Sixth-Seventh Ward in Salt Lake City when I served as bishop, came from Hamburg, where Hans Guertler served as branch president. Also from Hamburg there came to my ward the Henry Niemann family and Anna Bankowski and her son Ralph.

I went to the airport to await the arrival of Joseph Wirthlin and Hans Ringger, after which we rented a car and drove to a designated meeting place in East Berlin. We had the privilege to meet with Henry Burkhardt, president of the Freiberg Temple; Frank Apel, president of the Freiberg Stake; and Manfred Schutze, president of the Leipzig Stake. Our meeting covered an extensive agenda. First President Burkhardt explained that almost six hundred live endowments had been performed, along with the sealings to the various families who were endowed. He and his counselors are well into the work, and the temple is running smoothly. President Burkhardt indicated that on one occasion recently the heating unit for the water in the baptismal font had failed, and the water was ice cold. President Burkhardt turned to a young boy who was going to be proxy for some baptisms and said, "Are you willing?"

"If you are," came the reply.

So they cautiously walked into that cold font. The boy said, "At first I was real cold, colder than I had ever been; but then I caught the spirit of what I was doing, and I realized how much what I was doing would affect the life of another person in eternity, and I did not feel the cold water.

I was baptized for sixty-seven individuals. I shall always remember the experience and particularly how I felt."

The two stake presidents indicated that they had had many interested persons inquiring about the teachings of the Church, primarily among those who attended the highly successful open house which preceded the dedication of the temple. We discussed the contemplated stake center in Dresden and the progress made on the stake center in Leipzig, and we reviewed plans for additional buildings to house our members in the German Democratic Republic. We also cleared the way for Elder Howard W. Hunter to be the official visitor at the Leipzig stake conference the last weekend in October of this year. All in all, our six-hour meeting was most successful.

We returned to Berlin and then flew to Frankfurt, where I stayed overnight at the Wirthlin home.

FRIDAY, SEPTEMBER 6, 1985

Flew to London and thence to Hamburg, Germany. In Hamburg I was met by Joseph and Elisa Wirthlin. We went to the hotel and conducted a last-minute review concerning the program for the weekend.

SATURDAY, SEPTEMBER 7, 1985

After a morning of consultation with Joseph Wirthlin regarding matters in the European area over which he presides, I joined Brother Wirthlin and the priesthood leaders of the area for the priesthood leadership session of the Hamburg regional conference.

The priesthood leaders from the Berlin, Neumünster, Hamburg, and Hannover stakes were in attendance. The stake center in Hamburg was filled to capacity. The spirit of the brethren was felt by me and Brother Wirthlin. The Spirit of the Lord was shared by all. I felt complete ease in speaking through an interpreter, which is somewhat unusual. I found that I did not need to grope for words and that thoughts came to my mind regarding what I should say and tumbled forth without interruption as the spoken word. I acknowledge the inspiration of heaven in the presentations at this particular meeting. Joseph Wirthlin indicated he had never attended a better priesthood leadership meeting, nor one which was more inspiring, in his entire life. It was almost like putting water on an empty sponge, so receptive were the priesthood leaders to the messages which we General Authorities provided.

In the evening I participated in a most pleasant dinner with the stake presidents and their wives, after which a program was presented by the local members. The program was directed toward the history of the city of Hamburg and featured its quaint traditions.

SUNDAY, SEPTEMBER 8, 1985

Today we met in a large auditorium for the general session of the regional conference. I had the members of each stake stand so that there might be pride taken by those in attendance as pertains to their specific areas. Most grateful were the members from Berlin, who feel isolated in their situation in West Berlin, well within the territory of East Germany. The members rejoiced in meeting with their counterparts in West Germany and had a time of fellowship which was most enjoyable for all. A fine spirit prevailed throughout the meeting. The singing was magnificent. Klaus Hasse, Regional Representative and former president of the Dortmund Germany Stake, conducted the meeting.

He did so in a fine fashion. President Bach of the Hamburg Stake served as host and left no detail unattended. The German people are masters of detail and most precise in carrying out the instructions given them. I feel right at home in this culture.

I remained in Hamburg for the evening, while Joseph and Elisa returned to Frankfurt.

I ate alone in the restaurant of the hotel this evening and contemplated my long years of assignment to the stakes and missions in Europe. I reflected upon my association with Percy and Thelma Fetzer, who presided in the beautiful city of Hamburg. I thought, too, of the members of my ward who had come from Hamburg, including the Hans Guertler family, the Sigfried Guertler family, Anna Bankowski and her son Ralph, and the Henry Niemann family. The entire kaleidoscope of World War II passed in review, including the terrible fire bombing endured by the residents of Hamburg. It was a time for reflection and yet was a lonely time, for the spoken word did not accompany the review in thought.

TUESDAY, SEPTEMBER 10, 1985

This morning I presided at a seminar for the mission presidents and their wives of the European area. We had thirteen couples attending, in addition to Brother and Sister Wirthlin, Brother and Sister Hans Ringger, and me. The sessions were informative and productive.

In the evening we held a formal dinner at the hotel, followed by testimonies.

WEDNESDAY, SEPTEMBER 11, 1985

Today was a beautiful day in Salzburg, as was Tuesday.

After a full morning of meetings, we boarded a specially arranged sightseeing bus and took the delightful trip to Berchtesgaden. At Königsee, we boarded the electric-powered motor boats for the trip up to St. Bartholomew's chapel and the upper Königsee. It was a most pleasant experience. Tourists had jammed the area, so we did not depart from the boat; otherwise, we would, of necessity, have stood in line for perhaps an hour to catch a return boat.

I remained in Salzburg that evening, while most of the presidents, including the Wirthlins and the Ringgers, returned to their homes in Europe. I took a solitary walk through the beautiful Mirabel Gardens in the center of Salzburg. They are magnificent and so well maintained. I then walked across the bridge spanning the wide river which eventually makes its way to the Rhine. On the far side of the bridge is situated old town Salzburg with its many quaint shops. This is one of the most beautiful and unique tourist attractions in the world. I spent an hour or so just browsing and enjoying the experience of being in a city which I truly love.

THURSDAY, SEPTEMBER 12, 1985

Flew to Zurich this morning, where I caught Swiss Air flight number one to New York City and then Western Airlines nonstop to Salt Lake City, arriving at 8:30 P.M. It was a long but pleasant journey homeward.

SATURDAY, OCTOBER 5, 1985

Attended general conference, including the 10:00 A.M. session, the 2:00 P.M. session, and the 6:00 P.M. priesthood session.

My opportunity was to speak as the concluding speaker

of the afternoon session. I directed my remarks to the general topic of "Those Who Love Jesus." My introduction cited a bumper sticker which I observed on the bumper of a car in southern California as it wove in and out of the traffic patterns of the L.A. freeway. The message on the sticker contained these words: "Honk if you love Jesus." With this introduction, I proceeded to point out a proper way to show one's love for the Savior of the world.

I concluded by using the example of our faithful Saints in the German Democratic Republic and the miraculous way in which our Heavenly Father has responded to their need and many prayers, including the dedicatory prayer which I offered upon the nation, and has brought forward for their benefit a beautiful, dedicated house of the Lord, that they might receive their sacred endowments and sealing blessings. I recounted the experience of standing on an outcropping of rock between the cities of Meissen and Dresden on the morning of April 27, 1975, and asking our Heavenly Father to bless the people with the righteous desires of their hearts. I remember offering these words in the extemporaneous prayer: "May today mark the dawning of a new beginning of thy work in this land." I mentioned that at this juncture, far below in the valley through which flowed the Elbe River, a bell in a church steeple began to chime and the shrill crow of a rooster shattered the Sabbath silence, each event heralding the beginning of a new day. I felt warmth of sunshine upon my face and hands, even though my eyes were closed and an incessant rain had been falling all morning. At the conclusion of the prayer, I gazed heavenward and discovered that a ray of sunshine had penetrated the thick cloud cover, encompassing the small area where our group stood. It was an evidence to me that

Divine help was at hand and that our prayer had been heard by a loving Heavenly Father.

FRIDAY, NOVEMBER 1, 1985

Today I was in Germany for a busy schedule of executive meetings. Our first session was with our legal counsel from the German Democratic Republic, Herr Wunsche. In attendance, in addition to our legal counsel, were Henry Burkhardt, Frank Apel, and Manfred Schutze, the latter two brethren being our stake presidents of the Freiberg and Leipzig stakes, respectively. Presidents Wirthlin and Ringger were also in attendance.

The purpose of this meeting was to bring the situation current relative to our relationships with the government, the operation of the temple, and the further expansion of our building program in the German Democratic Republic. Herr Wunsche outlined for our benefit the fact that had the government known two years ago the great interest which the erection of a temple would have occasioned among the population of the German Democratic Republic, permission would never have been given for the erection of such a facility. We know the Spirit of the Lord prompted the timetable and that the temple has proven to be a great blessing to our members. In fact, the attendance is so great that it is necessary to reserve a place for many of the temple sessions.

I was heartened by the results of our meeting. It appears that the constitution of the German Democratic Republic provides a certain freedom of religion. Of necessity, religious organizations must be very careful in their observation of the laws of the land, particularly in this Communist-ruled nation.

118

Later in the afternoon formal sessions were held with Henry Burkhardt, Brother Apel, and Brother Schutze to discuss our past progress and future plans for the Church in that country.

Later in the day, a Brother Kirby Smith, district president from Athens, came to Frankfurt, where he joined us for a meeting regarding the future of the work in the nation of Greece. It appears as though the central European countries are beginning to be aroused with respect to an interest in religious matters. Perhaps this is our day of opportunity. As President Kimball often said, "If you can't get a foothold, get a toehold as we attempt to move the work forward." I am optimistic and feel confident relative to the future of the Church in these nations and in Europe in general.

SUNDAY, DECEMBER 8, 1985

Continued the leadership sessions for the priesthood leaders of German-speaking Europe. Also invited were the leaders from Holland.

After the instructional meetings were concluded, I held a lengthy session with Henry Burkhardt, Frank Apel, and Manfred Schutze, our leaders in the German Democratic Republic. The purpose of this meeting was to transfer responsibility from me to Russell Nelson, who will now be the first contact to Joseph Wirthlin for the countries of Eastern Europe.

It was most satisfying to me to note the progress made during the past seventeen years that I have had this particular assignment. We have progressed from oppression, restriction, and little, if any, printed literature to a position where the people have the full Church program, all the members are in stakes of Zion, a ten-building construction program is underway, and a holy temple of the Lord has been constructed and dedicated. I am grateful to the Lord and attribute all honor and praise to Him and to the faith of the membership which brought forth the miracle.

Later in the afternoon I met with Hans Ringger, Russell Nelson, and Joseph Wirthlin to transfer responsibility for Czechoslovakia, Yugoslavia, Poland, and Greece to Brother Nelson.

In the evening I went to dinner with Joseph and Elisa Wirthlin and Russell and Dantzel Nelson.

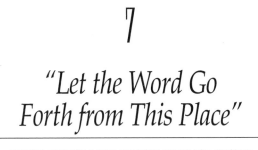

7

"Let the Word Go Forth from This Place"

**EAST GERMANY PREPARES TO SEND
AND RECEIVE MISSIONARIES
1986–88**

This morning we flew from New York City to London, after which we flew to Berlin, remaining overnight at the Schweizerhof Hotel.

Entered the German Democratic Republic today and drove to Leipzig, where it was our opportunity to meet with all of the priesthood leaders in the German Democratic Republic. They had assembled both from the Freiberg and the Leipzig stakes. It was a powerful group of priesthood brethren, filled with faith and devotion, with whom we met. The sisters, in the meantime, met in a special session, where Dantzel and Frances, as well as Helen Ringger, provided instruction. The Leipzig stake center, newly completed, is a beautiful building.

It was my privilege to dedicate the beautiful Leipzig German Democratic Republic Stake Center. This is a commodious and lovely building. It blends beautifully with the

We gather for dedication of the Leipzig stake center. Left to right: Elder Hans B. Ringger, Frances J. Monson, Inga Schutze, President Thomas S. Monson, Dantzel Nelson, Elder Russell M. Nelson, and Dieter Berndt.

German landscape and environment. After the dedication we went to the old building formerly occupied by the Saints in the Leipzig area. I hearkened back in memory to the day when Hans Ringger and I visited unexpectedly the Leipzig Branch, found the heating plant completely shut down because of malfunction and lack of parts, yet noted the spirit of our Saints as they sang, shoulder to shoulder, the songs of Zion, wearing their overcoats.

SUNDAY, AUGUST 24, 1986

This morning we met in general assembly in a lovely rented facility with all of our members from the German Democratic Republic. A wonderful spirit prevailed. Representatives of government were present, the hall was filled to capacity, and an expression of gratitude was seen in the countenance of each person present. The music was truly outstanding. At one point, the choir was joined by all of the children, who came from the sides of their parents and walked forward to the strains of the beautiful Primary song "Called to Serve." I noted that even the government officials had tears in their eyes when they saw this evidence of love as children joined the adult choir for the singing of the hymn "I Am a Child of God."

In a way, this was my valedictory address to the Saints of the German Democratic Republic. I recounted my eighteen years of service with this particular assignment and pointed out the progress which our Heavenly Father had provided them. It was a particularly touching occasion for me. I extended appreciation to Henry Burkhardt and his counselors for the work they had done through the years and further expressed gratitude to the two stake presidencies and to all of the General Authorities and Regional Representatives who had served this people.

After the meeting was concluded, we journeyed to the temple at Freiberg, where we stopped at the home of Henry and Inge Burkhardt for refreshments. This is a lovely temple president's home—perhaps the nicest home in the entire area. The weather was simply beautiful. The Lord blessed us abundantly.

In the evening we stayed at a beautiful hotel on the banks of the Elbe River. The hotel had been built by the Japanese in collaboration with the government of the

German Democratic Republic. We also visited the site in Dresden where ground has been excavated for the new stake center to be constructed in that city.

SUNDAY, OCTOBER 19, 1986

After a youth meeting at the Hyde Park chapel in England, Frances and I flew to Berlin, where we were met by Dieter Berndt, our Regional Representative. Together we crossed Checkpoint Charlie and were driven to the Hotel Metropol in East Berlin. Here we transferred cars, leaving the hotel chauffeur, and drove with Henry Burkhardt to our meeting place in East Berlin. I had the opportunity to provide the sealing power to two brethren and to set apart two new counselors for Brother Burkhardt, our temple president of the Freiberg Temple. We spent an hour or two with regard to instructions. I responded to questions pertaining to temple administration.

We then drove back to the checkpoint and to West Berlin, after changing cars once again to our Hotel Metropol driver.

TUESDAY, FEBRUARY 17, 1987

Attended the regular meeting of the First Presidency.

At ten o'clock I attended the Appropriations Committee meeting, where a lovely new building was approved for East Berlin. I worry about our declining membership in the German Democratic Republic but am aware that we have a window of opportunity negotiated several years ago which permits us to build up to ten buildings without further negotiation of a serious nature with the government. I feel it is our responsibility to take advantage of this opportunity and to construct the buildings and, at the same time, place increased emphasis upon member missionary work.

TUESDAY, APRIL 14, 1987

This morning I attended a meeting of the Appropriations Committee, where funds were appropriated for a beautiful new building in Dresden, German Democratic Republic. We have authority from the government to build ten buildings in that country. We have buildings completed in Leipzig, Freiberg and, of course, the temple in Freiberg. We are now moving forward for buildings in East Berlin, in Dresden, in Annaberg, and in other locations. My main concern in this country is the necessity of our members putting forth every effort in member missionary work so that our member base does not shrink as our population gets older but rather is replenished with converts as well as by births.

FRIDAY, SEPTEMBER 11, 1987

Today I had a pleasant hour with a bishop and his wife from the German Democratic Republic. Walter Hiller and his wife, Annie, served as my interpreters. At the conclusion of the visit, I took the bishop into the First Presidency's north boardroom and let him sit in President Benson's chair. He said it was an experience he will never forget. Once again I asked this good brother and his wife what his impressions were of our country. He said he was impressed by the size of our country, it being much larger than he anticipated. He was also impressed by the fact that Americans display freedom in saying what they want to anyone they choose without fear of government surveillance. When I asked the couple what food they preferred, unitedly they said, "The beautiful fruits and vegetables which you have in such abundance here in America."

TUESDAY, FEBRUARY 2, 1988

At ten o'clock this morning I attended a meeting of the Appropriations Committee, where a substantial sum was appropriated for the erection of additional buildings in the German Democratic Republic. I am happy that a break-through seems to be in the offing pertaining to having a lim-ited number of full-time young elders from the West serve as missionaries in this country. They would be located as guides at the various locations where we have buildings. This would be ideal and an answer to my real concern rela-tive to the future of the growth of the Church in that nation.

MONDAY, OCTOBER 24, 1988

Early this morning we crossed Checkpoint Charlie and entered East Berlin, where we were taken to a beautiful hotel and hosted to a delightful luncheon by Kurt Löffler, secretary of religious affairs for the entire German Democratic Republic government. Mr. Löffler, the host, was most cordial in welcoming us to the German Democratic Republic. I noted that the only drinks on the table were orange juice or water. This applied not only to the Latter-day Saints present but to all who were present. Others who were in attendance were Herr Behncke, assistant to Mr. Löffler, Herr Zeitl from the Ministry of Foreign Trade, and others. Brother Möller from the Una area of the German Federal Republic served as my interpreter. At one point fol-lowing the exchange of gifts and the conclusion of pleas-antries and dinner, Mr. Löffler escorted me to an open window where one could see the skyline of East Berlin.

With a gesture of his arm moving from far left to far right, he said, "Following World War II, as far as you could see from this position, only seven buildings were standing." He was obviously very proud of the rebuilding which had taken place in East Berlin. It is truly a latter-day miracle that Germany has been rebuilt following the extensive destruction of World War II.

At the conclusion of our meeting, we boarded our Volkswagen bus, driven by Hans Ringger, and made our journey through the rain to Dresden—a trip of just under three hours.

TUESDAY, OCTOBER 25, 1988

This morning we joined together and went to the site of the Dresden stake center. Here we had a complete tour of the building. I am so impressed with the fact that we now have a commodious stake center in the city of Dresden. The building also has quarters for our area office and is built after the European pattern, where quality dominates more so than in some countries.

After the tour of the building, we held a special meeting with government leaders, both national and local. An entire bus of dignitaries came from East Berlin, including Mr. Löffler, Mr. Behncke, Mr. Zeitl, and others. They brought beautiful bouquets of flowers, and as one of our leaders would speak, he would be presented with a bouquet on behalf of the government. It was a lovely occasion, and cooperation and appreciation for one another's beliefs seemed to dominate.

After the special meeting, luncheon was served for all who had assembled.

In the late afternoon we held a dedication service for the

membership of the Church. This provided me an opportunity to reflect on my twenty-year period of service to the people of the German Democratic Republic. I recounted some of the important events in this history, including the promise made at Görlitz twenty years earlier that if the Saints continued faithful in adherence to gospel principles, they would receive any blessing that any member of the Church would receive in any other country. Almost all aspects of the promises have been fulfilled. It is nothing short of a miracle that our membership of the Church in this country enjoy the blessings which they now do, including patriarchal blessings, the full Church program, and a beautiful temple dedicated and in use right in their midst. Every member of the Church in the German Democratic Republic is now a member of a stake—either the Leipzig Stake or the Freiberg Stake.

WEDNESDAY, OCTOBER 26, 1988

Very early this morning we drove from Dresden to Freiberg, spending the morning in the beautiful temple there. The damaged carpet has been replaced with a far more attractive and beautiful carpet. Henry Burkhardt and his wife, Inge, are ideal as president and matron of the temple. We had a choice time together.

We then journeyed to Zwickau, where we arrived in time for a tour of the new building for the Zwickau Ward, which tour had been especially arranged for the government workers and leaders who were present. At Zwickau, approximately six thousand people of other faiths attended the open house that preceded the dedication of the building. (In Dresden, the number soared to 29,740.)

Following the tour of the Zwickau building, a special

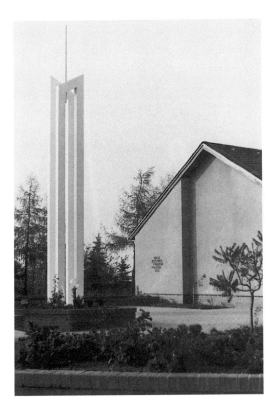

*The Zwickau chapel
at the time of its
dedication in 1988*

meeting and luncheon were held for those who were in attendance.

In the late afternoon as we prepared to dedicate the building, a humorous event took place. Most of the members of the area knew that their stake president, Frank Apel, had lost the ends of two of his fingers in a lawn mower accident. While the severed portions of the fingers had been restored, it had been a source of concern to all who knew President Apel. It appears as though he is making good progress in his recovery, once again enjoying the use of his fingers. On the lawn to the side of the chapel, there was a full-grown sheep tethered to a tree. The sheep had a sign tied about its neck that said, "President Apel's safe lawn mower." The sheep was actually given to President Apel. When I asked him what he was going to do with the animal, he said, "Oh, I'll take it home in my station wagon, of course." Everyone had an enjoyable laugh concerning this experience.

Once again the dedication ceremony was beautiful. The choir sang in an inspired fashion. Little children would walk up to their mothers and fathers who were singing in the choir and stand silently at the side of a parent while that parent performed as a member of the choir. I thought this showed respect on the part of the children and likewise love on the part of the parents and the children. We heard from the oldest member of the Church in that area, who had been a member since 1924. It was a time of rejoicing.

Following the dedication, a brother came forward and asked that I give his greeting to President Ezra Taft Benson, adding, "He saved my life. He gave me food to eat and clothing to wear following the war. He gave me hope. God bless him!"

We then drove to the city of Potsdam outside of Berlin and stayed at the Cecilienhof, a famous hostelry patterned after the British style.

THURSDAY, OCTOBER 27, 1988

Early this morning we assembled for breakfast at the Cecilienhof and then had a beautiful tour of the city of Potsdam. This is the city where the division of Germany was planned and approved following the termination of World War II. On the walls of the council room were the various proposals of the division of German and Austrian territory. We were shown the quarters where the Russians stayed and where the British were housed, as well as where the American contingent stayed. President Harry S. Truman represented the United States government, Joseph Stalin the USSR, and Winston Churchill and his successor, Clement Attlee, Great Britain.

Following the tour of the city, we reassembled at the Cecilienhof for a complete tour of this facility. Herr Wunsche then treated us all to a delicious luncheon in the dining hall, which had been occupied by the successful Allied powers years earlier. Frances was to have been here today but did not make the trip, feeling it might be a little too much for her. In her absence Herr Wunsche led the group in singing "Happy Birthday" to her.

I noted outdoors at the Cecilienhof grounds that the workmen, dressed as European workmen dress—in long, flowing smocks—were loading leaves on a wagon pulled by a beautiful horse. It seems as though the gathering of leaves in the old-fashioned manner symbolizes those traditions from which Europeans hate to depart.

We then drove to Berlin, where we were hosted to a dinner at the roof of the Grand Hotel, a magnificent hotel built by the Japanese to showcase the progress of the German Democratic Republic. The dinner was delicious. I was seated at the table with Herr Behncke who, I discovered, is a fisherman, as I am. In his conversation with me, Herr Behncke said, "I know you; I trust you. You and I can speak honestly as friends." He then said, "I believe some of the same principles you believe," and he made a comment regarding his wife and their long-term, successful marriage. He then said, "If I were joining a church today, I would join your church." I thought this highly significant.

FRIDAY, OCTOBER 28, 1988

This morning we held a planning meeting prior to our official state visit to the halls of government in the German Democratic Republic. I recalled how at one time the land we now know as the German Democratic Republic was the most productive area of the German-speaking world as pertained to missionary success. The city of Chemnitz, now known as Karl-Marx-Stadt, had as many as six branches of members and was the largest concentration of Latter-day Saints outside of North America. Then came the terrible destruction of World War II. After the bombs ceased and the artillery went silent, the land was left devastated. Then, like moles from the earth came the people, bedraggled, hungry, frightened, lost. A nation lay desolate and destroyed. About that time, the prophet of the Lord determined that one named Ezra Taft Benson would undertake a rescue mission to those people. President Benson left his dear wife and precious children and went on a mission, the length of which was left uncertain. He traversed the land of Germany—East and West. He fed the people. He clothed the people. But more than that, he blessed the people and gave them hope. I thought back to the time twenty years before when I received my initial assignment to supervise the work of the Church in Europe. At that time I had never been to Germany. I knew little concerning the history of the Church there. I did know, however, that the Cold War was on at that time. I knew that Americans were being arrested as spies on trumped-up charges and placed in jails. I knew that there were Soviet soldiers everywhere to be found, along with their dogs and machine guns. The Saints, however, had a wonderful spirit. They trusted in the Lord with all their hearts, and they leaned not to their own understanding.

At precisely the appointed hour we met with Erich

Honecker, the general secretary for the entire German Democratic Republic. Our cars had to arrive at the very minute of our scheduled appointment. We were then ushered into a large hall where we were accorded every courtesy and amenity. As we approached the meeting rooms, Herr Honecker and his delegation came forward to meet us. Our delegation was led by me and consisted of Russell Nelson, Hans Ringger, Henry Burkhardt, Frank Apel, Manfred Schutze, and Brother Möller. Herr Honecker had his deputies present, along with an able interpreter and his state secretary for religious affairs, Mr. Kurt Löffler. I presented to Herr Honecker a beautiful statue entitled *First Steps*, wherein a mother is bending over and steadying her child as the child walks to its father. Mr. Honecker seemed particularly pleased with this gift and emphasized that he advocates the strength of the family.

In our meeting chambers, we sat around a large, round table where once again the only beverages were orange juice and water. I simply can't get over the respect they show for our Church standards. Mr. Honecker began by making us feel welcome, saying that he had observed me and our Church activities for many years and that we taught our members to obey and sustain the law of the land and to be good citizens, that we emphasize the family, and that our Church members were ideal citizens of that land.

Chairman Honecker then gave me the floor to present my matters, although the matters which I was to present had previously been submitted to him, which is their custom, so that he and his associates are never taken unawares. I pointed out that the Church had been established in the German Democratic Republic for many, many years prior to World War II. I emphasized that this was one of the most productive areas for our Church missionary activities in all

the world at that particular time. I stated that our membership base is barely holding steady and that this concerns us.
I expressed appreciation for the cooperation of the government in granting permission to build the Freiberg Temple
and then related that at the open house events for our other
chapels and in Freiberg, large numbers of people have
stood in line to see our buildings and to inquire concerning
the Church. I mentioned that in Freiberg, almost 90,000 persons went to the open house; in Leipzig, about 15,000; in
Dresden, 30,000; and in Zwickau, 6,000. I indicated that we
really needed to seek from him his permission to recom-
mence the work of full-time proselyting missionaries in the
German Democratic Republic. I explained that these missionaries from other nations, when they come to his country and return to their homes, are advocates of the people
and the ideals of those people with whom they have
worked for two years. By way of illustration, I commented
that when the Argentine ambassador came to visit the First
Presidency, we were able to take him to Brigham Young
University, and there he met with about two hundred missionaries who had been in Argentina whom he could read-
ily observe were great advocates of Argentina and her
people. I then indicated that we would like to have permission for young men and women within the German
Democratic Republic to receive mission calls to serve elsewhere in the world and that this would be a broadening
benefit, both for the people with whom they labored and for
the young missionaries themselves.

Mr. Honecker, at the conclusion of my remarks, then
began to speak about his goals in government. For about
thirty minutes we heard from him that the German
Democratic Republic was really only forty years old and
that they had made remarkable strides in the reconstruction

following the devastation of World War II. For a moment I realized that I had been serving the people of that nation exactly half the entire life of the country—namely, twenty years out of forty. He then went on to point out that the embargo which our country had placed on technological materials had caused them a delay in the advancement of their nation. Obviously he didn't like this. He then indicated that this only stalled their program but that their own ingenuity had come to the fore and that they had been very successful in inventing new computer chips which may revolutionize the entire country.

He then proceeded to acknowledge our requests and said that in the future all of our young people could meet together in youth conferences, using state facilities if necessary, for he trusted our young people and admired them. This was a great compliment. He then reviewed my request for missionaries and simply said, "Permission granted. I will leave the details to my state secretary, Mr. Löffler. You can work them out with him; but permission is granted, both for missionaries from the outside to come here and for missionaries from our country to go elsewhere." This was the purpose of our visit, and success, through the help of the Lord, had been achieved.

Our meeting, which went for about an hour, also included compliments from me relative to the outstanding performance of athletes from the German Democratic Republic who participated in the Summer Olympics at Seoul, Korea. It also included a mutual agreement that the Lamanite Generation would again visit the German Democratic Republic in 1990. This performing group is very popular in that country. Most of the German people of middle age have read Karl May novels about the American West. While Mr. May never visited the American West, he wrote about it with the same vivid flourish as Zane Grey. However, in Mr. May's books, the Indians usually emerged victorious. The German people are absolutely intrigued by the American Indians and enjoy learning of Indian lore.

As we said good-bye, I thanked Mr. Honecker for his kindness and his understanding and assured him of our appreciation. As we went into the large hall, we signed the guest register and Russell Nelson turned to me and said, "Have you noted that while we have been in this country there has generally prevailed cloudy weather with rain, whereas at this point, when we've heard the good news concerning missionary work, the heavens have rejoiced and sunshine has enveloped all of us."

In a few minutes we were having a press conference outside the doors of the main government buildings. I noted by contrast the politeness of the reporters in the German Democratic Republic as compared to the general manner of reporters in America. Incidentally, Mr. Löffler and Mr. Honecker asked to have most of our visit covered by television, so we brought along a crew from KBYU who photographed all of those activities in which we participated, with the exception of the private meeting with Mr. Honecker.

In a few minutes we were across the border, the crossing being the most efficient that I have ever experienced. Once in West Berlin, we went to the airport and, after a period, took the plane to Leeds, England.

THURSDAY, NOVEMBER 3, 1988

Attended the meeting of the First Presidency and then the temple meeting. It was good to be back with the Brethren in the temple.

Later in the day I met with Elder Russell M. Nelson, as well as with Elder L. Tom Perry, chairman of the Missionary Executive Council, to plan a strategy for the opening of missionary work in the German Democratic Republic. We will have to move with care but also without delay in taking advantage of the opening that is now before us. I anticipate that many of the missionaries assigned to that country initially will come from among those currently serving in the other German-speaking missions. We would begin missionary work on a small scale and then hopefully move upward in number.

8

"Wilt Thou Intervene
in the Governmental Affairs"

**THE BERLIN WALL CRUMBLES
1989–90**

This morning I served as opening speaker of the ten o'clock general conference session. I gave a report of the history of the Church in the German Democratic Republic and was able to announce that three days earlier, on Thursday, March 30, the first missionaries to enter the German Democratic Republic in fifty years crossed the border, were met by their mission president, Wolfgang Paul, and commenced their labors. I further announced that the first ten missionaries ever to serve from the German Democratic Republic had received their assignments and would be going forward in other nations of the world as missionaries. For me it was a time of rejoicing and deep spiritual satisfaction.

SUNDAY, MAY 28, 1989

Ten missionaries—citizens of the German Democratic Republic—arrived in Salt Lake City today and journeyed to the Missionary Training Center at Provo, Utah, to prepare for their missions. They are the first from their country to

139

serve abroad as missionaries. Among the missionaries was Tobias Burkhardt who, as a young deacon, began caring for the grave of Joseph A. Ott, who perished as a missionary to Germany in 1896. Young Tobias had felt he would never have the opportunity to serve as a missionary, inasmuch as he lived in East Germany. Now he is here preparing for his service in the Utah Salt Lake City Mission. Asked about his feelings, he said, "I'm anxious to serve my mission. I'll strive to work ever so diligently, remembering the inspiration I felt each time I visited the grave of Joseph Ott."

THURSDAY, JUNE 29, 1989

The highlight of the First Presidency meeting today was the privilege to visit with the ten missionaries who are in the Missionary Training Center whose homes are in the German Democratic Republic. It is remarkable how rapidly these young men have learned the basics of English. They are fine appearing, and their attitude and exuberance for the gospel are evident in their countenances. All three of us—President Ezra Taft Benson, President Gordon B. Hinckley, and I—bore our testimonies to them and wished them well, invoking the blessings of Heavenly Father upon them in their missionary assignments. This is truly a miracle—that we have ten young men from the German Democratic Republic embarking on missionary assignments with the full blessing of the leaders of their government. In fact, a luncheon was held in their honor before they left their homeland, sponsored by the minister of religious affairs, Herr Kurt Löffler. The Saints in West Berlin also were there to meet them prior to their departure from the West Berlin airport.

Today the parents of one of the missionaries serving in

East Germany shared with me a letter they received from their son, Elder Anderson. I quote part of it here:

> You asked about the baptisms and the size of our wards. Well, our ward has about 76 members. We are, on an average, baptizing about seven to ten converts a month. This place is door-to-door heaven. Four out of five people invite us in and want to make an appointment. The people here are wonderful.
>
> Something very special happened to us the other day. As we were tracting, we ran across a school teacher. He was very interested in our message. We were invited to teach at the high school. He was very interested in our message. Today is Preparation Day. We just returned from teaching a group of students in this school about the Book of Mormon. Over 135 people were there, and so was the spirit. We have over 80 people interested in learning more about the Church and have invited all of them to see a video tomorrow night. The teacher was so impressed that he booked us for three more days of teaching. This will increase our contact pool to over 230 people.

THURSDAY, JULY 27, 1989

Today marks the beginning of the first joint youth conference for the young men and young women of our church in both West Germany and the German Democratic Republic. The conference is scheduled from July 27 to August 4. No other group has ever had authority to bring out of the East busloads of young people to fraternize in a constructive way with their counterparts in the West.

MONDAY, NOVEMBER 6, 1989

Today is marked by unrest in Eastern Europe. Large crowds began taking trains and automobiles to Hungary when the border between Hungary and the German Democratic Republic was opened. The people then gained passage to West Germany. Others did the same thing, using Austria instead as the intermediate point. Individuals by the thousands took this route to freedom, with no protest to speak of from the Hungarian or Austrian governments. In the German Democratic Republic, the people marched in the streets of Leipzig and then in Dresden, demanding more freedom and the ouster of the incumbent government. Marches also took place in other countries, such as Poland and Hungary, with the people demanding more freedom. There seems to be a great movement among the nations of Eastern Europe toward freedom.

THURSDAY, NOVEMBER 9, 1989

More movement toward freedom in the German Democratic Republic. Chairman Honecker has resigned, and many of his cabinet with him. Demands are being made for a full resignation of the government in power and the entry of the others appointed by free elections. There is a demand for the Berlin Wall separating East from West to come down. Once more Leipzig is a center of attention. Interestingly, we had received notification privately through Herr Löffler and Herr Behncke of the Ministry of Religion that Chairman Honecker would step down this week.

SUNDAY, NOVEMBER 12, 1989

Attended church services in our own ward. Once again word from the German Democratic Republic is that the people want more and more reform. The Berlin Wall is indeed crumbling, with more entry points being provided, with the citizens of the German Democratic Republic being permitted to go forward into West Berlin and indeed being provided fifty-six dollars of spending money by the West Berlin government, after which they return to their homes in the East. The prognosis is that the border will be opened and the repressive wall become less and less of a factor of separation. How will all of this affect the Church? I really believe no one knows at this point. We will simply have to wait and see. One thing is certain. The strong grip of Communism in these Eastern European countries is slipping as the people yearn for freedom and independence.

FRIDAY, MARCH 16, 1990

At 11:30 I met with the KBYU staff, under the direction of Bill Silcock, for an interview pertaining to my work in the German Democratic Republic. Television cameras and equipment were set up in the west boardroom, and the interview went forward. All of us are very much surprised by the rapid changes which have occurred in the eastern nations of Europe. The overthrow of Communism in the German Democratic Republic, in Poland, in Hungary, and in Romania has not been anticipated. The vacuum that now exists will provide for good leadership or despotic leadership to emerge. Let us hope that, step by step, democracy may come to these nations and that good leaders will emerge.

TUESDAY, APRIL 3, 1990

This evening Frances and I hosted a dinner for Mr. and Mrs. Gunther Behncke and President and Sister Manfred Schutze. The dinner was held on the twenty-sixth floor of the Church Office Building. General Authorities who have

I welcome Gunther Behncke, assistant secretary of religious affairs for the German Democratic Republic, during his 1990 visit to the United States. Left to right: Inga Schutze (wife of Manfred Schutze), Gunther Behncke, Mrs. Behncke, and President Thomas S. Monson.

had specific responsibility with the German Democratic Republic were invited, along with their wives.

Gunther Behncke spoke and delivered a masterful presentation. He spoke of the need of his country to emerge from Communism and now look toward the West. He flatly stated that capitalism had defeated socialism in the Cold War. He left us with no illusion that the pathway of the East Germans would be easy. He pointed out that during the period following the war, while the nation was ruled by Communist leaders, the people had been fed, they had been sheltered, and they had been clothed. Under a new regime he felt that while opportunities would be greater and freedom would be assured, there would be those who would suffer as the result of being deprived of food, shelter, and clothing.

As I spoke, I reminded the group that Herr Behncke had

Gunther Behncke, assistant secretary of religious affairs for East Germany, is honored at a dinner. Seated at far side of table, from left, are Gunther Behncke, President Thomas S. Monson, Frances J. Monson, Elder Hans B. Ringger, President Gordon B. Hinckley, and Marjorie P. Hinckley.

been very helpful to the Church in our building program, particularly in the erection of the temple and in our missionary efforts, being responsible in part for assisting us in opening the country to full-time missionary work and giving an opportunity to young men and women of that country to be full-time missionaries abroad. At general conference in my opening remarks, I had particularly welcomed government officials, including Herr Gunther Behncke from the Ministry of Religion of the German Democratic Republic. In the meeting this evening I added in German a particular greeting in which I said that we appreciated our dear brother and did so with all of our hearts.

At the conclusion of the evening, we presented Mr. and Mrs. Behncke with gifts, a small crystal ball of the world for him and a lovely statuette of a woman for her. Pictures were taken and music rendered. I believe each one present experienced an evening never to be forgotten.

I reminded the group that a year or two ago when I was meeting in East Berlin with the leadership in the religious ministry, Herr Behncke had leaned over to me and said, "If I were going to become a member of any church, I do believe I would seriously give thought to becoming a member of your church." When I mentioned this at the party, he nodded his head affirmatively, a little surprised that I had remembered the statement.

It has been our opportunity to host Mr. and Mrs. Behncke and to provide visits to Snowbird, Welfare Square, Temple Square, the canyons in southern Utah, the Missionary Training Center, the state government buildings, and so forth. We had also extended an invitation to Herr Kurt Löffler and his wife long before the government changes took place. I hope they will be able to journey to Salt Lake City at a future time.

TUESDAY, APRIL 10, 1990

Early this morning the First Presidency met with Gunther Behncke and his wife. Gunther Behncke is the secretary of the office that governs religious affairs in the German Democratic Republic. He is a civil servant who has served under a number of officers appointed to oversee religious matters. It was a lovely meeting. We took a picture of President Benson greeting Herr Behncke. President Benson commented upon his service in war-torn Europe, where substantial amounts of welfare aid were distributed to our starving members and to others.

146

WEDNESDAY, MAY 16, 1990

After meeting with the First Presidency, I placed a telephone call to the Freiberg Germany Temple. I extended calls to Brother Victor E. Cannon and Brother Rudi P. W. Lehmann to serve as counselors to Henry Burkhardt in the temple presidency. Henry has continued his work with his original counselors since they were called as counselors at the time of the dedication of the temple. Inasmuch as they are in their eighties and have served long and well, they were extended honorable releases.

SUNDAY, MAY 20, 1990

At seven o'clock this evening, KBYU presented *Fortress of Faith,* a one-hour documentary pertaining to the Church in the German Democratic Republic. The film depicts the significant events which have occurred since the conclusion of World War II and then the long road toward the full Church blessings the members now have. Of course, this spans my personal ministry to this part of the world and becomes a historical record of that ministry. The documentary is well done.

I am happy to have been a part of this most significant saga in the history of the Church in Germany. I acknowledge the hand of the Lord.

THURSDAY, MAY 31, 1990

This morning we flew to Berlin that we might have an opportunity to see the remnants of the Berlin Wall. To our surprise, we found that in most parts of Berlin, the wall was already gone. At the famous Brandenburg Gate area there was not even a trace of the wall. One could even see the old streetcar tracks which had been covered by the wall. The

Brandenburg Gate itself was under extensive remodeling and repair. It will soon mark the most famous gateway in Germany, replacing the notorious wall, which is now history.

This afternoon we took a boat ride down a small river, noticing the Berlin Wall still standing in areas beyond Berlin itself, although these remnants, too, will come down shortly. While we were cruising along the river, a patrol boat of East German police came by. Someone announced that this would be the last day that the river would be patrolled now that the two Germanys are moving toward reconciliation. All along the river route on the East German side, we noted house after house all boarded up and unoccupied for the long period that the wall has stood. This was due to the fact that the area behind the wall had to be cleared of any persons or commerce up to, perhaps, a fifty-yard length.

We stayed at the Schweizerhof Hotel in Berlin.

TUESDAY, JULY 3, 1990

Attended the regular First Presidency meeting and the Appropriations Committee meeting. I was pleased to note on the agenda of the Appropriations Committee the matter of a new mission home for the mission in Hungary and likewise consideration for a future site of a mission home in what is now East Berlin.

THURSDAY, OCTOBER 18, 1990

Before leaving to board the flight to London, I paused to reflect upon the fact that President Benson's improvement in health and return to his home permitted me the opportunity to participate in what will be one of the most significant gatherings in the history of the Church in Germany—the reunification of the units of East and West into one church within Germany. On October 3, just over two weeks ago, the two governments were officially reunited.

The flight to London went very smoothly. We then transferred to a plane going to Frankfurt, where we remained overnight.

SATURDAY, OCTOBER 20, 1990

This morning Frances and I departed Salzburg amidst the many clouds which filled the sky and foretold of rain later in the day. We feel fortunate that the day we had in Salzburg was a pleasant autumn day.

After arriving in Frankfurt, we changed planes and flew to Berlin. On approach to Berlin, I could not help but think of the many times I had flown into this historic city over the past twenty-two years, during which I have had some responsibility pertaining to the work of the Church in this part of the world.

Today marks a most meaningful event for me. Upon arrival in Berlin, Frances and I got into a taxi and asked the driver to take us to the Wall. He didn't move. My German is not very good; I tried again, and he still didn't move. Finally, he put his hands in the air and said, "The Wall is *kaput!* The Wall is *kaput!*" He drove us to where the Wall had been, and it was gone. A great change, a miracle, had occurred.

I met with Russell Nelson and Hans Ringger to put finishing touches on the planning for the conference.

In the afternoon, I attended a leadership meeting of all of the priesthood. There is no lack of priesthood leadership in Germany. In attendance were the priesthood leaders from the Berlin, Leipzig, and Dresden stakes. We then met with the men and women of the area. The spirit of our meetings was absolutely of the highest inspirational quality. Just to think that brethren from the East who have not had the opportunity to meet with their friends and family from the West are now being permitted to do so after a thirty-year period gives some idea concerning the emotional height which was reached. I couldn't help but notice the fact that the West Berliners were better dressed and had nicer automobiles but that those from the Eastern area, Leipzig and Dresden, if anything, had greater faith, speaking collectively.

SUNDAY, OCTOBER 21, 1990

This morning the Saints gathered from the Berlin, Leipzig, and Dresden stakes in a beautiful facility called the ICC, or International Congress Center. The attendance was 2,438.

A splendid choir provided the music. The German members truly sing with all of their hearts and put to shame the manner in which we sing our hymns here in Utah and other places in America.

I noted that Herr Gunther Behncke, minister of religion, and his wife were seated on the front row. Mr. and Mrs. Behncke had visited Salt Lake City earlier in the year and had a wonderful time being with us. He sang the hymns, and they both participated in the spirit of the occasion.

Hans Ringger, who is really one of the great moving forces in the expansion of the work in Europe, read for the approving vote of those assembled the changes which would put certain units from the Leipzig Stake into the Berlin Stake. In short, units from West Berlin and East Berlin will now be in one stake, and then certain units from the Dresden Stake were added to the Leipzig Stake, and certain units in the Republic of Germany were added to units in what formerly was the German Democratic Republic—primarily small groups of people in Nuremberg and the city of Hof.

At one point all of the children were invited to walk up the aisles of the beautiful building in which we were meeting and assemble in the front, comprising a children's chorus. They sang "I Am a Child of God." The children of American servicemen sang one verse in English, and the German children sang the next verse in German. The final verses were sung in German by all of the children. Every heart was moved.

Speakers on the occasion included each of the stake presidents: President Grunewald from Berlin, President Schutze from Leipzig, and President Apel from Dresden, followed by President Burkhardt, president of the Freiberg Temple. Russell Nelson and I were the concluding speakers. On the previous evening we had heard from Sister Nelson and Sister Monson and from Dieter Berndt and Johann Wondra, both Regional Representatives.

I spoke of the manner in which our Heavenly Father had blessed the work of the Lord in what once was the German Democratic Republic. I related specifics—that first visit in 1968 to Görlitz, where I was appalled by the fact that there was no opportunity for our members to receive their patriarchal blessings or to go to the temple. There was no privilege to print literature and lesson manuals; there were no visits from leaders of the Church from headquarters. Yet the gospel flourished through their faith and their reliance upon the Lord and upon one another. On that occasion I stood and, with a heart filled with emotion, promised the faithful Saints that if they continued to live worthily and to obey the commandments of God, every blessing that any member of the Church in any other country could receive would in time be theirs.

Almost without notice, and little by little, the blessing was fulfilled through the years. First, patriarchal blessings were provided by Percy K. Fetzer and Hans B. Ringger from other areas, and then Brother Walter Krause was ordained a patriarch by Spencer W. Kimball. I assisted him on that occasion. It is interesting that Brother Kimball said, "I ordain you a patriarch to give blessings to all worthy persons behind the Iron Curtain." Brother Krause reported to me that as of today, he has given 1,060 patriarchal blessings. Sister Krause acknowledged that she had typed every one of those blessings.

I then referred to the historic rededication of the land. I recounted the experience of standing on an outcropping of rock between the cities of Meissen and Dresden on the morning of April 27, 1975, and asking our Heavenly Father to bless the people with the righteous desires of their hearts. I remember offering these words in the extemporaneous prayer: "May today mark the dawning of a new beginning of thy work in this land." At this juncture, far below in the valley through which flowed the Elbe River, a bell in a church steeple began to chime, and the shrill crow of a rooster shattered the Sabbath silence, each event heralding the beginning of a new day. I felt the warmth of sunshine upon my face and hands, even though my eyes were closed and an incessant rain had been falling all morning. At the conclusion of the prayer, I gazed heavenward and discovered that a ray of sunshine had penetrated the thick cloud cover, encompassing the small area where our group stood. It was an evidence to me that divine help was at hand and that our prayer had been heard by a loving Heavenly Father.

The Lord has thus far fulfilled almost every aspect of that prophetic promise, culminating with a beautiful temple, chapels, all of the ordinances of the gospel, and finally, freedom. I acknowledge the joy I have had over the last twenty-two years in playing a part in the Lord's plans for His Saints in this part of the world. I also acknowledge freely the Lord's help and ascribe all honor and glory to Him.

The conference in a way marked the fulfillment of my specific assignment to the work of the Lord in this area. I am sure that over the years some of my brethren who have not been permitted to receive assignments in this area would like to have done so. I was able to have perhaps more than twenty of the Brethren assigned to district and mission conferences and then stake conferences over the years, but by keeping close to the work for this extended period, I was able to establish the continuity which developed trust on the part of government officials and resulted in our having missionary work permitted in the nation, which seemed to be the great breakthrough that preceded other blessings.

At the conclusion of the conference on Sunday, very few people wanted to leave. It was as though they were savoring the spiritual experience which had come to them during the conference. As we prepared to leave the auditorium, the chorus sang the beautiful number, "Auf Wiedersehen, auf Wiedersehen," which comes from the hymn, "God Be with You Till We Meet Again." It was one of the most spiritually satisfying weekends of my life.

In the remarks given by Dieter Berndt on Saturday evening, he related the experience he had as a bishop visiting with a rather reserved and quiet woman who resided in his ward. At length she told him of her difficulties—the loss of her husband and the loss of her children. As he was speaking, I noted how many men and women in the congregation withdrew their handkerchiefs and wiped tears from their eyes. It was as though their own personal experience had been revisited, and for a moment memories flowed anew as pertained to days gone by.

Following the meeting, a Sister Arndt, from the eastern section of Germany, came up to me and handed me a note expressing her gratitude. I include here her note:

> I was very anxious to talk to you while you were here, but there are so many people. Therefore, I am taking this opportunity to write to you. My son was called on a full-time mission to California. We are so happy and grateful he's worthy to do that, for with this, a prophecy for him and also for me was fulfilled. As his mother, I always strongly believed in that prophecy. You pronounced that prophecy for my son in Dresden, and I have kept your words always in my heart.
>
> My son was nine years old at the time you met him in Dresden. He and I were sitting there with grateful hearts. We were happy to have good seats. You, dear Brother Monson, gave a fine message and made our hearts feel good. You kept looking at my son, Thomas, and you smiled and said, "Here in front of me is sitting a young man with blond hair and brown eyes named Tom. He will serve a mission one day."
>
> My son Thomas was embarrassed at the time, but I knew that was a prophecy for him, and we've remembered it. He was often discouraged and sad in life because he was so very short of stature, but we knew what Heavenly Father now had in store for him. Now he is worthy to go on a mission—the fulfillment of his greatest wish.
>
> My dear husband was also baptized, thanks to our first

missionaries, after he had been an investigator for nine years.

I know you do not have much time. I'd like to apologize for having written this letter. I just wanted to share my joy with you.

In the evening we flew to London and stayed at the Marriott Hotel.

9

"With Thee All Things Are Possible"

AN APOSTLE'S PROMISES ARE ALL FULFILLED 1991–95

Late in the day Walter and Edith Krause visited the office. Edith had been brought to Salt Lake City by the sisters who organize the annual women's conference at BYU. I invited my secretary, Lynne Cannegeiter, to sit in on the discussion since she and her husband had been to Freiberg and other parts of Eastern Europe, and I felt she would be interested in Edith and Walter Krause's report. It was thrilling to hear how these two good people persevered through difficult times and helped to hold the Church together during the dark period of the Berlin Wall and the exclusion of missionaries from that country.

SUNDAY, MAY 5, 1991

In the evening I went to the Tabernacle and there met President Donald R. McArthur of the Utah Salt Lake City Mission and Elder Tobias Burkhardt. The priesthood restoration broadcast was planned to go by satellite to many locations throughout the United States and Canada and some locations abroad. The meeting featured a videotaped testimony of a deacon, a teacher, and a priest from different countries of the world, the young men being introduced by Elder Jack Goaslind, president of the Young Men organization and also a member of the First Quorum of the Seventy. This was followed by a message by Elder Marion D. Hanks, executive director of the Priesthood Department. He too used a clip from an excellent videotape on reactivating less-active Melchizedek Priesthood holders and those who hold no priesthood. Elder Dallin H. Oaks was also a speaker at the meeting, after which I was the concluding speaker.

I entitled my talk "Once a Deacon, Now an Elder." I attempted to address the need for advisers to catch the vision of their work and used as an illustration the manner in which Harold Watson served as adviser to the teachers quorum over which I presided. I told of a one-eyed pigeon that he effectively used by giving the pigeon to me, knowing that it would come back to his loft each time I turned it out. When I would go to retrieve my pigeon, I had a priesthood interview with my quorum adviser.

I then retold the story of young Tobias Burkhardt, pointing out that he was the East German lad who, as a deacon, cared for the grave of missionary Joseph Ott. Tobias, I mentioned, felt he would make a missionary contribution only in this way, citizens of the GDR not having any opportunity to leave their country. As I retold the story and mentioned the events that had taken place in the German Democratic Republic which permitted missionaries to come to America and missionaries from here to go to that nation, I commented that Tobias Burkhardt was one of the first ten missionaries to have that privilege to come to the Missionary Training Center in Utah and to then serve a full-time mission. In his case, he serves in the Utah Salt Lake City

Mission and is scheduled for release in just two weeks. Others of the ten served in Chile, Argentina, England, Canada, and the United States.

At the conclusion of my message and the retelling of the Joseph Ott story, I announced that the missionary who was then a deacon, namely Tobias Burkhardt, is now an elder, and I brought forth Elder Tobias Burkhardt to bear his testimony.

His presentation was most effective, as he thanked his parents and acknowledged the hand of the Lord in his life. His testimony was an encouragement for the young men who hold the Aaronic Priesthood to keep their faith in God alive and well, and that in due time, through obedience, our Heavenly Father's blessings will come. I felt good about the entire meeting and acknowledge the help of my Heavenly Father.

TUESDAY, MAY 14, 1991

At 1:00 I hosted a luncheon at the Lion House for Henry and Inge Burkhardt's son Tobias, who is rapidly coming to the close of his mission in the Utah Salt Lake City Mission. Accompanying Elder Burkhardt were fellow missionaries from the former German Democratic Republic at the Missionary Training Center in Provo, Utah, who were about to go forward on their assignments and a lady missionary working at the visitors' center at Temple Square. Others in attendance included Brother and Sister Joseph Wirthlin; Sister Thelma Fetzer, widow of Percy Fetzer; and their son, Clark. My secretaries also were in attendance, and Frances joined me for the event. It was a lovely occasion. We heard from each of the missionaries and wished them well on their assignments. Tobias was the first of the missionaries from the German Democratic Republic to receive a missionary call. He had despaired of ever having the opportunity to serve as a missionary, and as a deacon and teacher in the Aaronic Priesthood had tenderly cared for the grave of an American missionary to Germany, Joseph Ott, who passed away and was buried near Freiberg. Also in attendance were President and Sister Donald R. McArthur of the Utah Salt Lake City Mission. A fine time was had by all.

THURSDAY, MARCH 26, 1992

I had a most pleasant visit with Henry Burkhardt, my longtime friend who presided over our Church operation in the German Democratic Republic for so many years. He came with Herbert Klopfer, president of the Salt Lake Eagle Gate Stake and a former German national himself. It was a privilege to visit with Henry and to be brought up to date concerning his family and his work as a Church employee in Frankfurt. I do think that after serving as our leader in the German Democratic Republic for so many years and then as temple president, it is a little difficult for Henry to be employed in a more subservient role. I was happy to learn that Inge, his wife, is fine and that Tobias, their son, now works for Lufthansa, having completed his mission in Salt Lake City. Brother Dieter Uchtdorf, stake president of the Mannheim Germany Stake, was instrumental in helping Tobias obtain employment with Lufthansa. Brother Uchtdorf is chief pilot and senior vice president of Lufthansa.

As I visited with Brother Burkhardt today, I said to him, "I am going to give you an assignment—perhaps one of the most unique assignments you have ever received. I am asking you to visit with Brother Walter Stover. He is in his nineties and is not in good health. I don't think he'll be with us much longer. I want you to go sit by his bed and ask him to tell you about his life. He will enjoy the opportunity, and you will treasure the memory of your visit."

Brother Burkhardt said, "I will have to speak in German. It is the only language I know."

"Brother Stover will enjoy conversing with you in German."

Brother Burkhardt did visit with Brother Stover and told me later, "I left his presence a better man and more determined to serve our Heavenly Father than ever before."

SATURDAY, APRIL 4, 1992

Today we commenced general conference. During the interlude between sessions, I met with Ursula Masters and her husband. Ursula came from the German Democratic Republic and simply wanted to advise me how pleased she was with the progress of the Church there. She thanked me personally for the efforts I have put forth in this regard. Her son will complete his mission in the Dresden and Berlin areas this July, and she plans to return to her homeland to accompany her son on a little tour and then return to Seattle, Washington, where the family lives.

FRIDAY, SEPTEMBER 25, 1992

I had a lovely visit here in Salt Lake City with Brother and Sister Werner Adler from Plauen, Germany, and their friends, Brother and Sister Schneider. We enjoyed the opportunity to visit together. Brother and Sister Adler were scheduled to come at Church expense some years ago to attend conference. This was through our program that provided for new bishops and their wives to come one time to a general conference. However, when their visa was applied for, a rejection resulted, inasmuch as they had no children, and the government policy then was to allow only those who let their children remain behind receive such visas, thereby guaranteeing the return of the parents. How pleased I am that the Adlers have now had an opportunity to visit Salt Lake.

FRIDAY, OCTOBER 2, 1992

At half past ten this morning, I had the privilege to meet with Tobias Burkhardt, son of Henry and Inge Burkhardt. As an employee of Lufthansa Airlines, he was able to fly to Salt Lake City without cost to him. He brought to the office with him a lovely blonde-haired girl whom he had met in Salt Lake City. I think they are rather fond of each other, but they have only known one another for such a short time that they are going to let a little time intervene before determining how serious the situation is between them.

I then met with the Rudolph Lehmann family. What a delightful experience to see Brother and Sister Lehmann with their three stalwart missionary sons who have together completed their missions in the United States. A mission would have seemed impossible to these young men just a few years ago, but through the intervention of the Lord, this privilege has become a reality. The Lehmanns are from the Chemnitz area, formerly a part of the German Democratic Republic.

TUESDAY, OCTOBER 6, 1992

This evening Frances and I hosted a dinner party at the Lion House for visitors from the former German Democratic Republic. Those included were Werner Adler

Left to right: Frances and I welcome Rudolph and Ruth Lehmann and their three fine missionary sons, Michael, Mattias, and Peter, in October 1992.

and Sister Adler; a couple from West Germany who accompanied the Adlers; Rudolf and Sister Lehmann from the former German Democratic Republic, who came to Salt Lake City to meet their missionary sons upon their release; the Lehmanns' three missionary sons, Michael, Matthis, and Peter; Klaus and Arleen Lassig of Salt Lake City; Brother Lassig's brother and his wife, also of Salt Lake City; Elder Joseph Wirthlin and Sister Wirthlin; and Bill and Lynne Cannegieter. Gerry Avant of the *Church News* took photographs and wrote a story.

The Lehmanns' three sons had served simultaneously in three U.S. missions: Michael in the Idaho Boise Mission, Matthis in the Tennessee Nashville Mission, and Peter in the Colorado Denver Mission. What a reunion this was for the missionaries and their parents! Following the meal, I called on each one of the missionaries to speak and also each of the visitors from Germany.

It is quite a miracle in and of itself to have had missionaries serving in the United States who were called from the German Democratic Republic, to say nothing of three missionaries from one family. They are outstanding young men.

SATURDAY, MAY 1, 1993

This morning very early, on a 6:18 A.M. flight, we returned from San Diego to Salt Lake City, arriving in time to prepare for and then officiate at the wedding ceremony of Tobias Burkhardt and his bride, Tannya Lorre Booth. Henry Burkhardt and Inge, parents of the groom, were in attendance, as were the parents of the bride. Tobias's only sister, in fact his only sibling, and her husband had come from Germany along with her parents to be present. The ceremony went forth in one of the older rooms in the Salt Lake Temple, room 5, and a sweet spirit prevailed.

As I performed the ceremony, I let my mind go back to the time when Tobias was an Aaronic Priesthood boy, caring in a quiet way for the grave of Elder Ott. It was very moving at that time to consider that this boy who could not hope to go on a mission or marry in a temple felt closer to God by performing that service for a former missionary's plot at the cemetery. Then the Lord took charge of things in the German Democratic Republic. The result was the removal of the wall and, prior to that, the building of a temple and chapels and a continuation of good relationships with the government, and then a mission right here in Salt Lake City for Tobias Burkhardt, and now marriage for time and eternity in the Salt Lake Temple.

*Tobias Burkhardt
and Tannya Booth,
just prior to their
wedding in the
Salt Lake Temple*

I have learned from my experience that man's extremity is but God's opportunity. I am a living witness of how the hand of the Lord has been made manifest in watching over the members of the Church in what once were Communist-ruled countries.

SUNDAY, MAY 29, 1994

Erich Honecker, former head of the German Democratic Republic, passed away today at the home of his daughter in the land of Chile. Erich Honecker was the principal architect of the Berlin Wall, which was built to stem the outflow

165

of freedom-loving people and skilled artisans from East Germany, their desire being to reside in the western portion of Germany where a democratic government led the people. Ruthless tactics were devised to prevent anyone from crossing the Wall—these tactics including death without trial administered by the guards who carefully patrolled and monitored the area leading up to the Wall from the East German side.

SATURDAY, SEPTEMBER 10, 1994

This morning we took the plane to Frankfurt and thence to Leipzig, Germany. It was interesting for me to fly into Leipzig, something I had never before done, having traveled there by automobile during the many years that I covered this area. You could see the old terminal, ancient and decrepit, and then a modern terminal, although small in size.

We were met at the airport by some of our leaders and were taken to the hotel and then to the Leipzig stake center for a wonderful session of conference. The building was filled to capacity, with 596 in attendance. The missionaries saw the conference on video in a room in the basement.

I had suggested that the opening song be one I heard in Görlitz on my first visit to the old German Democratic Republic. In the Sunday School hymnbook of years ago, it was called "If the Way Be Full of Trial, Weary Not," with the chorus beginning, "Do not weary by the way." The Germans sang with tremendous enthusiasm. They seemed glad to see me, and I was overjoyed to see them. Tears could not be restrained as the memories flowed through my mind, and my heartfelt gratitude welled up within me concerning all the blessings they had received and how our Heavenly Father had answered our prayers in their behalf.

*Edith and
Walter Krause*

The conference was one ever to be remembered. Walter and Edith Krause were in attendance, sitting on the stand. I had Walter tell the congregation how many patriarchal blessings he had given to Saints behind the Iron Curtain. I think the total was about 1,080, and Edith had typewritten every one of them. I asked all those who were in attendance when I first spoke in that general area if they would raise a hand. I was surprised at the great number who have come into the Church or who had been born and reared in the twenty-plus years I had the assignment who had, of course, not been present when I first went there in 1968.

In the evening we returned to the hotel.

SUNDAY, SEPTEMBER 11, 1994

Early this morning we left by car for Dresden. A beautiful day had dawned. The sun was shining, and it was a pleasant drive for one and a half hours to the beautiful city of Dresden. We went immediately to the hotel and then to the stake center for a one-session stake conference. Henry and Inge Burkhardt accompanied us, as did Brother Wilfred Möller from Dortmund, who has for years been my interpreter.

What a contrast to go to the stake center, which I had the privilege to dedicate, and compare it, with its commodious rooms and bright and appealing atmosphere, to the old theater where we once met. Once again the singing was truly out of this world. I marveled at the congregation. They knew that my emotions were near the surface, and they wept freely during the service. There were 945 in attendance.

In my remarks both at Dresden and at Leipzig, I attempted to point out how they had been the recipients of the guiding hand of the Lord. All in all, the Lord opened His basket literally and bestowed upon them, beyond their finest and dearest expectations, His abundant blessings.

I mentioned a youth conference I had attended and how I had brought four or five cartons of Wrigley's gum and had given each one of the young people a stick of gum as a memento, they having never seen Wrigley's gum. A mother of two or three little children saw me in the foyer and said, "I was one of those young people to whom you gave a stick of gum. I will never forget that meeting."

Also as I went downstairs to speak to the missionaries after the conference, there was a large young man on the front row. As I had each one introduce himself, I said to him, "You're a large man. I'd hate to guard you on the bas-

We enjoy a glorious visit to the site in Friedensburg, just above the Elbe River, where the land was dedicated and rededicated in 1975.

ketball court." I noted he had a fine suit upon him which fit him very well. I later learned it was one of the suits I had given to Brother Adler, and he in turn had given it to the missionary, who did not have adequate clothing.

I noticed a lady standing by a wall in the foyer and felt impressed to talk to her before going into the missionary meeting. She was from Bulgaria. We had a very pleasant visit. I later received a handwritten letter which she had penned and left to be delivered to me. She wrote that she was seeking from the Lord knowledge as to whether true apostles were on the earth today. She had made somewhat of a pact with God that if I were a true apostle, I would stop from wherever I was going and pause and talk to her about her Church membership. I am so glad this was the prompting I received, for in her mind and in her heart, she then said she had a testimony that I was a true apostle and that the authority was on the earth once again.

After dinner, we went to the old cemetery where there is situated the grave of Joseph Ott. We noticed a number of other graves where the stones had the replica of the Freiberg Temple. We discovered that these were widows and others who had died and who had wanted to be buried in the little cemetery nearest where we once met in the old theater. I learned that after a period of years, the graves are dug up and the headstones discarded if perpetual care or continuing financial care for the grave is not made available. I just cannot imagine the disruption of a sacred grave of a sweet, faithful Latter-day Saint simply because she has no heirs to pay for the upkeep of the grave. I am sure we could do something to prevent such an event from occurring to any Latter-day Saint who is buried in that cemetery.

We then went to the area where I had offered the dedicatory prayer upon the land of the German Democratic Republic on April 27, 1975. We walked to the outcropping and, in full sunlight, looked at the beautiful scene that I had witnessed those many years before. The Elbe River flowed as serenly as ever; Dresden and Meissen were on the various sides of one's view, and a sweet feeling permeated the place. Our little group had assembled, and I mentioned what had been spoken that day and how the promises had all been honored and fulfilled by our Heavenly Father. I suggested that we offer a prayer of thanksgiving, which I did.

We then returned to our automobiles. I felt I would like to return to the spot, and Brother Neuenschwander, sensing that I was uncomfortable, said, "Brother Monson, would you like to go back to the spot alone?" I said, "That is exactly what I am thinking." And I went back to the spot and meditated and personally thanked God for His watchful care of these choice people. The presence of the Lord was very near. It was quiet. The surroundings were beautiful, with no one to intrude or disturb. I looked heavenward as I expressed my thanks aloud in the simple prayer and received a spiritual confirmation that the prayer had been heard and the gratitude had been accepted.

We returned to the hotel, where we had a light supper and enjoyed a stroll around the beautiful city. The old theater where we once met is now a Chinese restaurant, and the area has deteriorated. Not one Russian trooper did we see, as compared to the throngs of soldiers that I had witnessed on such visits all through the first twenty years of my visits to that country. Peace and freedom had returned to our Saints in Germany.

SATURDAY, AUGUST 26, 1995

This morning we took the plane to Dresden, Germany, checked into our hotel, and then, with Brother and Sister Dieter Uchtdorf, drove to the temple in Freiberg, where we spent a most delightful evening. It was so good to see President and Sister Jiri Snederfler. Jiri has been temple president here for four years. Their assignment will end as of September 1, when Brother Justus Ernst will become temple president.

I remember so many years ago sitting at the kitchen table in Brother and Sister Snederfler's home in Prague, Czechoslovakia. Those were difficult times. Everybody was being watched, but they never feared. I will always remember Sister Snederfler turning the pages of her missionary scrapbook. It contained photographs of missionaries who had been about twenty years old at the time the pictures

171

were taken. She would look at a photo and would say, "Oh, wonderful boy." These many years later, as I sat there with her, these "boys" were now middle-aged men.

She pointed to one missionary in the book and said, "Here is a wonderful young man."

I said, "I know him. His name is Richard Winder." Neither of us could imagine that before too many years had passed, Brother Winder would be presiding in the Czechoslovakia Prague Mission.

I must confess that in the home of the Snederflers, I saw more pictures of the temple than I have ever seen in my life. I think I counted twelve, and I said to Sister Snederfler, "I have never seen so many pictures of the temple."

She took me into an adjoining room and said, "Here are more."

I said, "I think your husband loves the temple."

And she said, "I, too. I, too."

Who would have thought then that the Snederflers would be presiding one day in the Freiberg Temple. It was a joy to be with them.

SUNDAY, AUGUST 27, 1995

This morning early we went by car to Görlitz, Germany. We stopped en route and visited the grave site of Elder Joseph A. Ott, that early-day missionary to this area about whom I have written earlier. Three weeks after his marriage in late 1895, Ott was called on a mission to Germany. While disembarking from the ship in Germany, he slipped and fell into the cold water. He was rescued, but days later he became very ill, and on January 18, 1896, one month and six days after his arrival in Germany, he died from black diphtheria. He was buried in the St. Pauli cemetery in Dresden.

172

The Görlitz chapel, dedicated in August 1995, stands as the final fulfillment of promises given to the oppressed East German Saints during one of my early visits.

August 1995:
Frances and I
revisit the grave of
Joseph A. Ott.

Later a tombstone bought with donations from German Saints was placed on the grave site.

I am happy to say that the local members have responded to my appeal and made sure that perpetual care is maintained for any of our members buried in the private cemetery there. Otherwise, after a given period of years, the headstones are removed, the remains placed in a mass grave, and the cemetery plot sold again. I don't want that to happen to any Latter-day Saint buried there.

At the site of the beautiful Görlitz chapel, we were met by the lord mayor, Matthias Lechner. He is a young man with a sweet spirit. I could not help but compare his visit with the absence of such kindness when I first went to Görlitz twenty-seven years earlier. Then there were informers in the audience, fear in the hearts of all the citizens, the presence of Russian troops in full military regalia, and East German police with their machine guns at their sides and their Doberman and German shepherd dogs straining at leashes.

It was here in Görlitz that I made a sacred promise many years ago that if the Saints remained true and faithful to the commandments of God, every blessing any member of the Church enjoyed in any other country would be theirs. That night so long ago, as I realized what I had promised, I prayed fervently that the promise would be fulfilled in the lives of those noble people. How grateful I am for the goodness of our Heavenly Father to his faithful Saints.

During the meeting today, the lord mayor spoke and presented a contribution for the maintenance of the building. It was a touching moment for me. As I looked over the audience, I saw many of our old faithful leaders, even those who were in attendance twenty-seven years earlier. Today marked the final culmination of the promise, which has been fulfilled gradually over the past twenty-seven years— even the dedication of a beautiful chapel in the very city where the promise was given.

After an hour or two of warm embraces and fond remembrances, we returned to Dresden. En route we stopped at the special place where I had dedicated and rededicated the land long years before. It was the same kind of day, misty and rainy, as we walked down the lane toward the mountain outlook. As I reminisced with those present concerning the events of that earlier period, the sun burst forth with all its splendor as it had done on the day of dedication. The Elbe River far below in the valley flowed ever onward as it has done through the years, in both good times and bad.

At Dresden we boarded the plane en route to London. Gratitude filled my heart and soul for the privilege of seeing the hand of the Lord in the blessing of this choice people.

Faith had been rewarded.

I enjoy a moment of solitude during a recent visit to the sacred site where the land of Germany was dedicated and rededicated in 1975.

INDEX